TRAINS
OF THE WORLD

Edited by Pat Hornsey
Editorial Consultants: Brian Hollingsworth and Geoffrey Kichenside

NEW ENGLISH LIBRARY
TIMES MIRROR

Copy Editor: William J. Howell

Art Editor: Deborah Miles
Designer: Nykola Stoakes

This edition published in 1979 by
New English Library Limited
Barnard's Inn
Holborn
London EC1N 2JR

© Text and illustrations copyright
New English Library Limited 1979

Set in 9/11pt Monotype Univers by
South Bucks Typesetters Limited
Printed by Fratelli Spada,
Ciampino, Rome, Italy

450 03599 9

Contents

Introduction

Trains have something about them that makes men love them. Sometimes – perhaps after too close an acquaintance – people hate them, but this is usually aimed at a railway in particular rather than trains in general. Finding the reason for this love is rather a puzzle; perhaps there is a clue in that it is almost wholly a masculine enthusiasm. Just as puzzling is the fact that the railway disease – incurable but seldom fatal – strikes so randomly, hitting families which have no railway connection just as frequently as those who do have one, or some members of a family but not others. Easier to understand is the many forms which the illness can take.

First, there are the nuts-and-bolts men, who like to know piston sizes and frame thicknesses of locomotives that were scrapped before they were born. Then there are historians, who worry whether it was 10 May or 11 May 1852 that the railway came to Puddleby-on-Sea. The collectors of insignia, nameplates and other railwayana are fairly ruthless in pursuit of their prey; while collectors of tickets have a pastime whose charm lies in the fact that tickets are supposed to be collected from you not by you.

Run your own railway? Yes, it is possible in scales from caterpillar to rabbit size; or, build and drive your own locomotive in sizes from $2\frac{1}{2}$-inch to $7\frac{1}{2}$-inch between the rails. Again, you can help to run a full-size railway; hundreds of organisations, with mileages from two or three up to tens of thousands, occupy the time of over ten million people the world over. Most get paid for it, too.

Train Timers are another fanatical group, who watch the mileposts and not the scenery. Books and books have been filled with their strange, dull but space-filling offerings. Even so, they do at least travel by train, unlike the camera fiends, festooned with the tools of their trade, who range the world but see more of the roads than the railways, because you cannot photograph trains if you travel in them. Still, it is their work that has made this book possible.

There are also the signalling nuts and the track-layout men and the number takers, but to all these specialists must be added as many more who just like trains . . . appreciating steam traction with its moving limbs and glorious sounds (even if there is not enough light to take pictures) but at the same time admiring the tireless efficiency of today's box-like traction units. Perhaps they would also agree that good food becomes excellent and indifferent food acceptable, provided it is taken in a railway dining-car. They delight in such facts as that the distance between the rails is that same odd 4ft $8\frac{1}{2}$in in both Darlington and Pekin – provided the spikes haven't worked loose. How clever of George Stephenson to have, as it were, patented the standard gauge in this way – if a more logical dimension had been chosen, anyone could have claimed to have originated it.

But whatever your speciality – and the writer confesses to having indulged in most of them – there is nothing to be lost by widening the horizon geographically and this is what this book is about. It also appears at a sad moment for the train lover in that in one sense it is a requiem. The reason is that the most evocative of all the elements which have gone to make a railway, that is, the steam locomotive, is rapidly phasing out. Twenty-five short years ago, the steam locomotives of British Rail would stretch, if placed on the same track, from London almost as far as Crewe; now all are gone, except for a few in pleasure use. The 20,000 or so that remain in the world are a vanishing species; indeed, by the time these words are printed, fires will have been finally dropped on a sizeable proportion of even this vestigial remnant. This rarest of all wild game is accordingly receiving special attention from the ferro - equinologist (student of the iron horse) in these its final years.

India is Number 1 in steam today, with a fleet approaching 10,000 in strength. The locomotives' construction and style are of enormous variety, spanning the years from Victorian times to the 1970s. In size they vary from tiny narrow-gauge tank engines to giant broad-gauge express locomotives. But go quickly – a giant off-shore oilfield has been discovered near Bombay.

The silver medallist is China, a country which has perhaps (the actual number seems a state secret) half as many steam locomotives in use as India. Most of them were constructed after the rest of the world (except India) had ceased building steam. Indeed, new ones are even now coming off the production lines at Tatung Locomotive Works, specially built for mass production of the March Forward class 2-10-2s; alas, this cannot last, but steam will be around in China for a while yet. Accordingly, Chinese steam is very modern and fine, but naturally there is little variety. Also, it is hard to get at; casual tourism is not a thing that the Chinese encourage.

South Africa gets the bronze; on the narrow-gauge metals of the Republic there still continue running giant locomotives, beautifully kept, which are bigger and heavier than anything that ran on standard gauge elsewhere, other than in North America. Until recently, young English railway enthusiasts of the 'total' variety used to go to South Africa specially to gain steam foot-plate experience; an activity that was possible because of a quirk in the white-black segregation laws. Strange, isn't it that the three top countries in steam – the four-figure men – are poles apart politically?

The amazing variety of ancient and modern steam which survives in Indonesia – with a low rate of diminution – only misses a medal by a photo-finish. As a steam sanctuary, it certainly rates the highest of the also-rans; and by all accounts Java and Sumatra are the pleasantest of countries to visit.

Of other countries which have fair quantities of steam, handiest to Britain are East Germany and Poland, provided one can accept the restrictions, inconveniences and tiresomeness of totalitarian regimes. The Germanic traditions of steam construction, so recently extinguished in West Germany, flourish in both these places. In this area, diminution is steady but continuous. The Germanic steam locomotive is also very much to the fore in Turkey, which also comes in the 'fair quantity' category. The rate of change in Turkey may be slower, but it is still relentless.

Notable as containing areas of the world still not

yet fully explored, South America hides away in its remoter corners some interesting pockets of steam, particularly still in Argentina. Most are run-down and diminishing fast, but remotest of all (a day's flight from the nearest hotel) is not far from Cape Horn at a location rather than a place called Rio Gallegos, where steam brings coal from mines far inland down to the ships. It is a model of its kind and, if its principles had been applied elsewhere, steam might still be performing the same function in many more places than Patagonia, where it does so.

East Africa, whose railways have just separated out into Kenyan, Tanzanian and Ugandan systems, still just swims in the steam world. In Kenya, on the Mombasa-Nairobi main line, can currently still just be found the most powerful steam locomotives running in the world today. These are the '59' class 4-8-2+2-8-4 Garratts; it is possible that they will still be there when the printer's ink is dry on the pages of this book.

Of other countries, Hungary must be singled out on the grounds of quality rather than quantity. A little steam, beautifully maintained, is still kept for a few low-utilisation duties. They have chosen for survival the most suitable regardless of age and, hence, fine modern 4-8-0s rub shoulders with centenarian 0-6-0s, already old when the Emperor Franz Josef was on the throne of the old Empire.

Portugal is another country where it is a race with the printer whether the present or the past tense should be used to describe its steam. There just is (or, just was, as the case may be) steam, of a particularly choice kind, on one or two of the lovely little narrow-gauge branches leading out of the Douro Valley in north Portugal.

Next in this sad tale of the decreasing use of steam comes a number of countries in which a handful of steam locomotives survive with remarkable persistence. Usually they perform some kind of stand-by service, either to cover diesel failure or to deal with occasional special working such as ballast trains or, on request, nostalgia trains for railway enthusiasts. Bulgaria, Czechoslovakia, Italy, Romania and Yugoslavia are examples of countries where the iron horse exhibits qualities of unpredictability and shyness (not to speak of preventive activities on the part of its game-keepers) that would do credit to an okapi or giant panda. Hence the charm of the steam safari.

Steam traction is now a matter for historians and museum keepers in Australia, Canada, France, Japan, the Netherlands, New Zealand, Switzerland, Spain (except for one tiny independent railway), United Kingdom, United States, West Germany and many other countries. The steam locomotive itself seems to have gone the way of other means of transport as it became obsolete; like the horse and the sailing ship, it has turned into an instrument of pleasure. Perhaps, one day, former Prime Ministers will spend five-figure sums on steam locomotives instead of sailing yachts; and Royalty will attend railway functions as regularly as they do the Badminton Horse Trials.

So steam is going and this is very sad. Railways, however, are not. Indeed, for the first time for many years one can say that there is a secure future for the iron road and not be accused of wishful thinking. Disenchantment with the motor car together with the uncertain future of oil supplies and many other factors all point towards a means of transport that is already adapted to other sources of energy. This is why, with almost no exceptions, every country in the world is showing faith in railways by modernising them, extending them or both. Even countries that have never had railways are considering joining the railway club.

As we all know, British Rail is putting 125mph High Speed Trains into service, with an 150mph Advanced Passenger Train to follow shortly. France has a new high-speed *railway* under construction between Paris and Lyons, while Japan is boring a tunnel for her high-speed network to connect the islands of Honshu and Hokkaido almost three times as long as the Simplon. Venezuela has begun on a 2,600-mile national system; in railway-less Afghanistan one is in the planning stage. New underground railways are springing up (if that is the right term) in cities from Caracas to Newcastle-upon-Tyne.

On many railways, less spectacular but equally important advances are taking place in other, perhaps more fundamental, things. Heavier jointless (welded) rail and concrete sleepers, heavily ballasted with great depths of broken stone, are transforming track conditions, while new electric signalling transforms operations.

Standard containers, transferable onto lorry or ship, bring the railway to any factory door or farm gate, as well as connecting the rail systems of all the continents. They are forming a steadily increasing proportion of railway traffic. In the background one notes computers of immense versatility being used more and more for the management and control of freight movement.

To adapt is not to perish; and wherever railway explorers go there will be lots for them to see, not only for those of our own but also, it is devoutly to be wished, for those of our grandchildren's generation.

B. Hollingsworth

Brian Hollingsworth

Australia

Australia, the 'Island Continent', has an area of nearly three million square miles — almost as great as that of the United States of America, nearly three-quarters of the area of the whole of Europe and about twenty-five times as large as Great Britain and Ireland. Powers of government are vested in six sovereign States, plus a Commonwealth Parliament, to which certain specified powers were transferred when the States agreed to form a Federation in 1901.

All these facts are important when we come to study the history of railway development in Australia. For, in this large country with a comparatively small population (just over fourteen million in 1978), there are not one, but seven independently - operated government - owned railway systems and three main gauges of rail track — 3ft 6in, 4ft 8½in and 5ft 3in. (In 1978, the Australian National Railways Commission took over long-distance rail operations in the States of South Australia and Tasmania, thus reducing the number of controlling authorities to five.) In South Australia there are considerable mileages of all three main gauges. The government

systems in Western Australia (Westrail) and Victoria (Vicrail) operate two gauges, and these are remnants of former narrow gauge (2ft and 2ft 6in) government lines in Queensland and Victoria. The problem of differing gauges in Australia has become well-known throughout the world, and has plagued railway operations ever since the lines of two adjoining systems met, in 1883.

But at the time when railway communication was first established in the Australian States, each was a self-governing independent colony of Great Britain, free to make its own choice on transport policy. The story of railway progress in Australia, therefore, can best be told by looking at each system in turn, and drawing the threads together at the end, as has been done, almost literally, with new construction since 1945.

In the early 1830s, coal companies in New South Wales drew on English practice by using horse-operated railed ways for moving coal to loading staiths in the Hunter river. Convicts provided 'push power' for a five-mile line on the notorious Tasman peninsula in Tasmania for a period after 1836. In May 1854, a horse-

1. First standard-gauge train through Avon yard (near Northam) from Merredin to North Fremantle in November 1966 hauled by a pair of Western Australian Government Railway's class K diesels. (*Western Australian Government Railways*)

2. A Queensland Government Railway's PB15 4-6-0, one of a class of more than 200 locomotives built from 1900, takes a passenger train over Stoney Creek on the Cairns Railway in north Queensland. The 'grandstand car' coaches had deep windows on one side and seats in tiers so that passengers could enjoy the view. (*M. C. G. Schrader*)

worked railway was opened between Goolwa and Port Elliott in South Australia — it was lengthened a little but remained isolated and horse-worked for thirty-one years. Thus the first steam-operated railway on the continent, the first of the lines which became railways as we know them today, was in Victoria — a separate colony since 1851.

Australia's first railway was built to link Melbourne, capital of Victoria, with its port of Sandrige (now Port Melbourne), three and a half miles away. The Melbourne and Hobson's Bay Railway Company was incorporated in 1853. Engines, rails, rolling stock and machinery were ordered from England. Construction was completed well in advance of the expected arrival of the engines. To avoid a delay in the start of the service, a local contractor was commissioned to build an engine – which he did, in the space of ten weeks at a cost of £2,500. The opening took place on 12 September 1854. The gauge of the line was 5ft 3in, which was adopted by other companies building lines to other Melbourne suburbs and became the 'standard' gauge for Victoria.

By 1864, railways linked Melbourne with the important centres of Geelong, Ballarat, and Bendigo, forming 200 miles of main trunk route. The line to the New South Wales border on the Murray river at Woodonga was completed in 1873; ten years later, the NSW line reached Albury on the northern shore, and a connection was made. For the first time, Australia's break-of-gauge problem manifested itself – passengers and goods had to change trains at the border.

Early Victorian locomotives, mainly of 0-6-0 wheel arrangement for goods working and 2-4-0 for passenger, were built in England. By 1873, the Phoenix Foundry at Ballarat was producing engines locally, sometimes to a 'pattern' engine from overseas. With the expansionist boom of the '80s, the Railway Commissioners introduced a degree of standardisation and five new classes containing some interchangeable parts, and design features needed for Victorian operation, were introduced, and the locomotives developed a distinctive appearance. The Railway workshops at Newport built their first locomotive in 1893, and were largely instrumental in

providing heavier and more modern power after 1900. The DD and A2 classes, both 4-6-0s, preceded heavier Consolidation and Mikado types for goods working, while four three-cylinder Pacifics were the pride of the passenger fleet up to the outbreak of war in 1939.

The 180 or so modern steam engines built after the war, including seventy R-class 4-6-4s of new design, had a comparatively short life; when dollar funds became available, Victoria embarked on dieselisation. Various American General Motors designs with components built in Australia under licence form the backbone of the present fleet of some 330 locomotives. As on all government-owned systems in Australia, Victoria's traffic is now handled entirely by diesel or electric power. In all States, however, some steam engines have been retained to please enthusiasts or tourists.

Passenger rolling stock in Victoria has tended to blend English and American design features. Four- and six-wheel carriages were replaced by bogie vehicles, the first of which appeared in service in 1862, and which became more widespread after 1874. Longevity has been a feature – some suburban carriages built in 1880 were lengthened in 1910-15, adapted for electric traction, and were still running in the early 1970s. The Melbourne suburban railways were electrified, after wartime delays, from 1919 onwards, when the first electric train in Australia left Melbourne for the suburbs of Essendon and Sandringham. Electrification to the heart of the brown-coal-producing areas in the Latrobe valley, 110 miles from Melbourne, was inaugurated in 1954-55.

The honour of opening the first steam railway in Australia nearly belonged to New South Wales. Before any decisive move was made in Victoria, the Sydney Railway Company was formed by an Act of 1849 to build a line of railway south and west from Sydney. A series of financial difficulties hampered construction for five years and, in the event, the government acquired the undertaking on 3 September 1855, twenty-three days before the official first train ran over the thirteen and a half miles 4ft 8½in-gauge line. Thus, the first NSW railway became the first State-owned steam railway in the British Empire. The constructing contractor, a Mr William Randle, operated the line under licence from a newly appointed board of commissioners for the first twelve months. Service was started with four 0-4-2 locomotives supplied by Robert Stephenson, and thirty-two carriages and fifty-seven goods wagons, all from England.

As the oldest of the railway constructing bodies in Australia, the Sydney Railway Company accepted the advice of its Irish engineer, a Mr Shields, to adopt the Irish 'standard' gauge of 5ft 3in for its Sydney-Parramatta line. The Victorian and South Australian governments agreed to the proposal and rolling stock for the Melbourne-Sandridge and Goolwa-Port Elliott lines was ordered accordingly. Shields resigned; a Scot – James Wallace – was appointed to replace him and persuaded the Sydney Railway to adopt 4ft 8½in for its track. As no rolling stock had been ordered, the directors agreed, and from that small beginning, Australia's rail gauge muddle began.

After its acquisition of the Sydney

1

Railway Company, the NSW government assumed responsibility for most railway construction in the State, where early builders faced tremendous problems. The city of Sydney is surrounded by rocky plateaux and mountain ranges, the ascent of which required great engineering skill. Chiefly responsible for overcoming those problems was Mr John Whitton, appointed engineer-in-chief in 1857. He fought and won a battle to build full-scale railways instead of narrow-gauge horse-worked tramways and even today many of his engineering works are in constant use. He was responsible for the design and construction of 2,100 miles of railway during his thirty-three years of office.

Progress out of Sydney was slow. The escarpment of the Blue Mountains presented a barrier to the settlement of the rich Bathurst-Orange area which was finally broken when Whitton designed two zig-zags for carrying the line over the range. The more spectacular, the Great Zig-zag near Lithgow, achieved world fame when it came into use in 1869; its three graceful sweeps carried the line down into the valley on a grade of 1 in 42. Increasing traffic forced major expenditure on tunnelling and regrading to eliminate the zig-zag in 1910, but its stonework is preserved today as a national monument. A 3ft 6in gauge steam-worked tourist line has been laid over part of the original route.

The years 1880-85 brought great progress in the railway network, with 1,000 miles of new lines constructed. But Sydney and Newcastle remained unconnected by rail, although the gap had been narrowed to a four-mile ferry journey along the Hawkesbury river. At last, in May 1889, a 2,900ft rail bridge over that river was opened, linking Sydney and Newcastle, and making possible a through rail journey from Adelaide to Melbourne, Sydney and Brisbane – albeit with two gauge changes en route.

Long distances are a feature of travel in NSW, and at an early stage night-time mail passenger trains became an established pattern of service. In consequence,

2

1. A New South Wales' class-36 4-6-0 pilots a Beyer-Garratt on a heavy freight climbing 1 in 40 at Borenore, NSW. The class-36 engines lasted almost until the end of steam in the State. (*M. C. G. Schrader*)

2. Victoria Railway's R-class 4-6-4 on a special passenger train in northern Victoria in April 1971. The R-class engines were the only 4-6-4s in Australia. They were built in 1951-2 by North British Loco Co in Glasgow. No 707, depicted here, was maintained for a time in the early 1970s for excursion trains. (*M. C. G. Schrader*)

3. A pair of 830-class 3ft 6in gauge Goodwin-Alco 900hp diesel-electrics of South Australia Railways leaving Cockburn yard for Peterborough and Port Pirie. (*M. C. G. Schrader*)

3

sleeping cars were introduced quite early, in 1877, and eventually formed a large fleet for the inter-colonial expresses and other night trains. Only in the years since the Second World War have higher-speed day trains tended to supplant night trains on premier passenger services.

As with most other Australian railways, the NSWGR relied mainly on English sources for early locomotives, but by the 1870s local builders were at work, including the railways' own workshops. Clyde Engineering later became a prominent supplier and the American Baldwin company a regular supplier. Continuing capacity for hard work, endurance and success have characterised a number of NSW locomotive types, and some must be mentioned. The P6 (later C32) class 4-6-0s, designed by newly appointed locomotive engineer W. Thow, in conjunction with Beyer Peacock in England, were first introduced in 1892. Over a period of nineteen years, a total of 191 was supplied by four different builders. They were extremely successful and versatile, handling express, goods and mixed trains with ease. One of them hauled the last regularly steam-hauled passenger train in NSW in 1971, not specially selected but on regular roster. For goods working, Thow introduced the T524 (later D50) class 2-8-0s in 1896. The 280 engines of this class, complemented by 190 of the improved D53 and 120 of the D55 class, became the standard goods engines of NSW.

In 1925, the first of twenty-five D57 three-cylinder 4-8-2s was brought into service for heavy goods working. Their tractive effort was sixty-seven per cent greater than the standard goods engines, but high axle loads restricted availability. The increasing weight of passenger expresses brought about the displacement of the C32s, firstly by two successful classes of 4-6-0 C35s and C36s. For the heaviest long-distance trains, the C38 class 4-6-2s entered service from 1943. Of the thirty engines, the first five were streamlined, and the entire group gained the respect of professional railwaymen and enthusiasts throughout Australia. In 1971, class leader No 3801 ran from Sydney to Perth over the new standard-gauge lines hauling an enthusiast special, and became the first locomotive ever to cross the continent in steam. In 1952, the NSWGR placed in service the first of forty-two AD60-class 4-8-4+4-8-4 Beyer-Garratts, the most powerful steam locomotives in Australia, and among the largest of their type in the world. One of these, No 6042, was the last steam locomotive to work in regular service on an Australian government-owned railway, in February 1973.

The mainstay of the present locomotive fleet are Alco-designed diesel-electrics of various classes. The twenty 40-class units introduced in 1951 are now all out of service in NSW, although some were reconditioned and sold to a mining

railway in Western Australia.

The first steam-operated line in South Australia linked the capital, Adelaide, with its port, and opened for traffic on 21 April 1856. Construction took place under government control, after private enterprise had failed in an earlier attempt to build the line. Three 2-4-0 engines named *Adelaide*, *Victoria* and *Albert* were imported from the Fairbairn company in England to begin the service. Originally, the track was laid with bridge rails, screwed and bolted to longitudinal sleepers, on the Great Western or Brunel system, but it proved unsuitable for the climatic conditions and the track was relaid with conventional cross-ties (sleepers) in 1868-69.

In South Australia, railway development first proceeded northwards from Adelaide. The copper-mining town of Burra was reached in 1870 by a 5ft 3in-gauge line, which was extended to Terowie by 1880. The first section of what is now the main Interstate line to Melbourne was opened as far as Aldgate, twenty-two miles, in 1883, and continued to the Victorian border by 1885. The Victorian Railways reached that point in 1887, and a through rail service over the one gauge from Melbourne to Adelaide became possible. The Intercolonial Express, as it was termed, included examples of the first rolling stock to be jointly owned by two Australian railway systems, and to this day the same practice is followed. The modern Overland express, with its sleeping, sitting, cafeteria and lounge cars, is jointly owned by the two

State governments.

In the late 1860s, the South Australian government made a momentous and unfortunate decision that future rail expansion in light-traffic areas would be built on the 3ft 6in gauge. No fewer than eight such separate railways originated at ports on the State's coastline. They finally merged into four major systems, the first of which, later known as the Western system, opened with a horse-operated line from Port Wakefield in 1870. Steam replaced horses in 1876. The Northern division originated at Port Pirie in 1875, and was built in stages to Petersburg (now Peterborough) in 1881.

Following the discovery of minerals at Broken Hill, the South Australian government built a line from Petersburg to the NSW border at Cockburn, whence a privately owned 'tramway' ran on to Broken Hill. This line was destined to carry millions of tons of ore concentrates from Broken Hill to smelters established at Port Pirie. The South Eastern narrow-gauge system based on Kingston opened in 1877, and the Port Lincoln division started operations in 1907. The government built and operated a line south from Darwin to Pine Creek, 146 miles, in 1889 and pushed a line of rail northwards through the desert to Oodnadatta by 1890. These two sections were intended to meet ultimately as a north-south link.

South Australia, therefore, faced major break-of-gauge problems within her own state borders. It eventually converted the Western system to 5ft 3in gauge, by 1927, and the South-East division by 1959. The

Port Lincoln division remains an isolated 450-mile 3ft 6in-gauge stronghold, but the busy Cockburn-Peterborough-Port Pirie line was converted to 4ft 8½in gauge in 1970. So South Australia today possesses major segments of railway on three different gauges.

Locomotive development on the South Australian Railways was characterised until the 1920s by a proliferation of types and classes. Most notable on the 5ft 3in-gauge lines were the eighty-four Rx-class 4-6-0s, built by English and Australian builders in the period 1886 (as R-class) to 1915. The 3ft 6in-gauge lines employed a series of 2-6-0 locomotives of increasing size and power as their mainstay of operation until 1903, when the first of seventy-seven T-class 4-8-0s made their appearance.

Motive power — and indeed the whole operating practice of the SAR — underwent a major change from 1923 with the appointment of Mr W. A. Webb as Commissioner for Railways. Webb had had extensive experience in the USA and the SAR became largely Americanised. A big-engine policy produced some powerful machines on the 5ft 3in gauge; notable were ten 500-class 4-8-2s for express working through the extremely difficult Hills section of the Interstate line; ten 600-class Pacifics for passenger work on flatter terrain; a series of 2-8-2s of the 700 and 710 classes for heavy freight working; and latterly a group of 2-8-4s for the same purpose. A lighter series of Pacifics, the 620-class, were built from 1930.

But motive power was only part of the plan. Bogie freight rolling-stock and caboose-type brakevans were purchased. Large-capacity high-speed coaling plants were installed at the main depots. Central train control was introduced on the main South line in 1924, and later extended. On light-traffic lines, train orders replaced the British-based staff-and-ticket system of safeworking common throughout the rest of Australia. Automatic signalling on both double and single lines replaced block working and electric staff where traffic was heavier.

It was an exciting, visually rewarding, and worthwhile change which has continued to influence South Australian thinking through to the present day. The SAR introduced its first diesel-electric locomotive — an Alco-based unit in 1951, and the system is now totally dieselised. Of interest is the fact that one class of diesel-electric, the 830-class Goodwin-Alco 900 hp locomotive, operates on all three gauges in South Australia — 3ft 6in, 4ft 8½in and 5ft 3in.

In March 1978, the South Australian Railways, as such, ceased to exist. Country services in that State are now operated by the Australian National Railways, Central Division. Adelaide metropolitan services are operated by the State Transport Authority — Rail Division.

The pattern of railway development in Queensland differs somewhat from that in other States, and reflects the manner in which settlement itself grew along the Queensland eastern seaboard. Self-government of the colony in 1859 was

followed by a demand for rail transport; the first line was designed to connect Ipswich with the fertile Darling Downs district. Political pressure influenced the choice of Ipswich, about twenty miles upstream from the capital, Brisbane, as the starting point rather than the capital itself. Through connection to Brisbane awaited the building of a river bridge in 1876.

On the recommendation of an Irish engineer, Abram Fitzgibbon, the gauge of 3ft 6in was adopted for the new line, which opened as far as Bigge's Camp (now Grandchester), twenty-one miles, on 31 July 1865. Surmounting two significant climbs, the Liverpool range and the Main range, the line reached Toowoomba, principal city of the Darling Downs, on 1 May 1867.

There followed a period when unconnected railways developed along the east coast. The hinterland from Rockhampton was tapped with a thirty-mile line of 3ft 6in gauge in 1867. Construction of the Great Northern Railway westwards from Townsville began in 1880 and the line reached the mining centre of Charters Towers in 1882. From Maryborough and Bundaberg, small sections of line opened

New South Wales' C38 No 3801, with two water-tank wagons, spares/workshop van, CR coaches and NSWGR sleeping-cars, forming an enthusiasts' special in October 1972. Two years earlier, in August 1970, this engine made the historic first and last through steam journey right across Australia from Sydney to Perth, a return run of about 5,000 miles. (*M. C. G. Schrader*)

in 1888; Cooktown and Mackay followed in 1885.

In 1887, work started on the Cairns railway. Construction of the fifteen-mile Barron Gorge section proved to be the most arduous in all of Queensland, and even today a journey over the line is one of the most spectacular in all Australia. There are fifteen tunnels ranging from fifty-six yards to 470 yards in length; the longest is approached on a $7\frac{1}{2}$-chain radius curve, has a 5-chain curve in the middle and a 15-chain curve at the other end. Six steel bridges and fifty-nine wooden trestles complete part of the story. From the top of the range, about 300 miles of 3ft 6in-gauge line was built by the Chillagoe Company to serve its mining interests on the Atherton table-land.

The joining of these independent coastal rail systems was a gradual process. Rockhampton was linked with the southern system in 1903, and a special Act of 1910 authorised the building of a north coast line through to Cairns, completed in 1924. Vast distances and a relatively small population have contributed to the operating problems of the Queensland Railways over the years. The system had the greatest route-mileage (approximately 6,600) of any State. Since the Second World War, closures of minor branch lines have been almost balanced by the laying of new track to serve vast mineral projects and, in 1978, the route mileage was approximately 6,100. The image has changed dramatically in the last ten years.

For use on the first section of line, the Queensland Government ordered four 2-4-0 engines from the English firm of Slaughter Grunning (which became the Avonside Engine Company soon afterwards). The diminutive machines weighed only twenty-two tons and produced a tractive effort of 4,500lb. They were soon joined by a later group of twenty-two-ton 0-4-2 Neilson engines, one of which was later sold to a private sugar-milling firm and saw out almost a full century of service. It was returned to the QGR for participation in its Centenary and eventual preservation. Not so successful were three double-Fairlie 0-6-6-0s brought out in 1867, and returned to their builders as unsatisfactory.

In earlier years, the QGR purchased locomotives from Baldwin in America and various English sources. For light lines, the 4-6-0 type ultimately found favour; 112 Class B13s were built from 1883 onwards and ninety-eight Class B15s introduced for goods working in 1889. Even more ubiquitous were the 202 Class PB15 passenger 4-6-0s with 4ft driving wheels introduced in 1900 and a further thirty of similar class developed in 1924. Kitson, of Leeds, built twenty of the originals; all the others came from Queensland firms, including the QGR's Ipswich workshops. The PB15s remained in service until 1969, when all steam

traction finished on the QGR (except for special workings). An extremely successful 4-8-0 for goods working, the C17 class, was introduced in 1920 and totalled 227 engines; the last were built after 1945. For heavier passenger trains, the B18¼ class 4-6-2s were introduced in 1926 and eighty-three were completed. An improved BB18¼ was first built in 1951. Other recent steam locomotives included thirty 4-8-2+2-8-4 Beyer-Garratts, and twelve 4-6-4Ts to augment the fleet of suburban tank engines in Brisbane.

Diesel-electric traction first came to Queensland in 1952 and spearheaded moves to increase the system's capacity and operating performance. For long-distance country services, nine air-conditioned all-steel trains have been built since 1953. The QGR developed railcar services more extensively than any other system, and eventually replaced many of them with modern stainless-steel units in 1956; where secondary passenger services survive, they are railcar operated.

The QGR formerly operated trackage of two other gauges, but the 2ft Innisfail Tramway, originally a passenger and general cargo carrier, was sold to two sugar-mills in the area in 1977. A sixty-

nine-mile 4ft 8½in-gauge line runs direct to Brisbane from the New South Wales border, but rolling stock is provided by the NSWPTC. This line was an early successful attempt to minimise break-of-gauge problems.

Australia's smallest State, the island of Tasmania, has the smallest route-mileage of railway, but there are fascinating aspects to its history. Private enterprise built the first line, from Launceston to Deloraine, to a gauge of 5ft 3in; it opened in February 1871. The Launceston & Western Railway Company, however, ran into financial difficulties and was taken over by the government in 1872. The Tasmanian Main Line Railway Company, another private venture, built and operated a 3ft 6in-gauge line from Launceston to the capital, Hobart, opening throughout for traffic in 1876. For the last nine miles into Launceston, a third rail was laid on the Launceston & Western's track and dual-gauge operation continued until 1888, when the latter was narrowed to 3ft 6in.

On the island's west coast, the Van Diemen's Land Company had laid a forty-four-mile 3ft-gauge wooden-railed horse tramway inland from the port of Burnie on Emu bay to the tin mines of

1. Break-of-gauge station at Marree on the Central Australian line, at left a north-bound NM 4-8-0 and at right a Commonwealth Clyde-GM diesel-electric. (*M. C. G. Schrader*)

2. A WAGR G-class 4-6-0 No 123 on a train of vintage carriages crossing the Capel river in 1968. Although the design dated from the 1890s, an engine of this class was the last steam locomotive to be at work regularly in Western Australia as late as 1973. (*M. C. G. Schrader*)

3. QGR Beyer-Garratt of 1951, No 1006 at Rockhampton shed in 1964. These engines were used on both express passenger and freight haulage and lasted until the end of regular steam services on QGR in 1969. (*M. C. G. Schrader*)

4. Two Sulzer-engined diesel locomotives of Commonwealth Railways haul a goods train into Alice Springs. (*M. C. G. Schrader*)

Waratah. In 1844, the Emu Bay and Mount Bischoff Railway Company took over the line and relaid it with steel rails to 3ft 6in gauge. The Emu Bay Railway Company, formed in 1897, extended the line fifty miles to Zeehan.

The government-operated 2ft-gauge North-East Dundas Tramway was notable both for its spectacular scenery and for its contribution to world locomotive development. Over its metals from 1910 were operated the world's first Beyer-Garratt locomotives; they were diminutive thirty-three-ton machines with 0-4-0+0-4-0 wheel arrangement, designed to negotiate curves of $1\frac{1}{2}$ chains radius and to climb gradients of 1 in 25. The two engines continued in service, intermittently from 1929, until 1938-39, when the tramway closed. Number 1 was restored in 1947

and shipped back to the works of Beyer Peacock in Manchester, England; when the works closed the relic passed into the care of the Festiniog Railway.

From Queenstown to Regatta point, the Mount Lyell Mining and Railway Company operated a spectacular twenty-one-mile line, including four and a half miles of Abt-system rack. The line was opened throughout in 1899 but closed as a result of high costs in 1963.

The Emu Bay Railway operated large Beyer-Garratts, each using two firemen to maintain steam on the continuous heavy gradients. The company was the last stronghold in Australia of a far-from-successful machine known as the Australian Standard Garratt. In an attempt to increase quickly the locomotive power available to meet wartime needs on

3

4

Australia's 3ft 6in-gauge lines, sixty-five 4-8-2+2-8-4 119-ton Garratts were built to a new and unproved design in railway workshops throughout Australia. The locomotives operated for varying periods in Queensland, South Australia, Western Australia and Tasmania. The Emu Bay bought two in 1948 and two more from Tasmania in 1961; they lasted until diesel-hydraulic locomotives replaced steam on the line. On 1 March 1978 the Tasmanian Government Railways became the Tasmanian Region of the Australian National Railways.

Settlement in Western Australia came more slowly than in the eastern States, and it was the development of the State's natural resources which first created a demand for rail transport. Timber milling led to the building of the first lines from Lockeville to Yokonup in 1871, and from Rockingham to Jarrahdale, near Perth, in 1872. The former used the first steam locomotive in Western Australia — *Ballarat*, built by the Phoenix Foundry in Ballarat, Victoria, and now preserved in Busselton.

The first government railway in the State was built to assist industry, this time lead and copper mining. Opened in 1879, the line ran from Geraldton, a mid-northern port, to Northampton. The gauge finally adopted was 3ft 6in, which was adopted as standard. Perth, the state capital, was connected by rail with its port of Fremantle, ten miles away, in 1881 and the line continued inland to Guildford. It formed the first section of the Eastern railway, which continued through the Darling ranges to York by 1885.

Two major railways in WA were built under the Land Grant system, by which private investors were granted ownership of land in return for building a railway through it. A London syndicate built a 243-mile line from Beverley (extension of the York line) to Albany on the south coast, opening in 1889. The Great Southern Land Company worked the line until 1891, when it was taken over by the government for £1,100,000. The venture had had mixed fortunes; public opinion led to the government takeover. While construction of the Great Southern Railway (as it became known) was in progress, another agreement was signed for a line from Midland junction (near Perth) to Walkaway (near Geraldton), a distance of 277 miles. Lack of capital on the part of the original grantee brought about formation of the Midland Railway Company of WA, which took over and opened the line in 1894 and continued to operate it until 1964, when the State took over.

The pattern of locomotive development in WA is complex — a striking mixture of the conventional and the experimental which has persisted to the present era. The first WAGR engines, two M-class 2-6-0s built by Kitson, of Leeds, epitomised English narrow-gauge locomotive practice of the time, and were used in building the Geraldton-Northampton railway. For work on the completed line, the Government imported two double-Fairlie articulated locomotives from the Avonside Engine Company, of Bristol, one of which was later converted to a 2-4-2 tank engine. Three single-Fairlie 0-6-4Ts were purchased from New Zealand Railways in 1891, but did not achieve the success hoped for in surmounting the grades of the Eastern Railway. In their place, a series of small-wheeled K-class 2-8-4T engines was designed. For general purposes, WAGR utilised 2-6-0 and 4-6-0 engines in the early stages, typical of many such locomotives throughout the Australian 3ft 6in-gauge systems.

In 1912, six 2-6-0+0-6-2 Beyer-Garratt locomotives (class M), the first 3ft 6in-gauge Garratts in the world, were ordered from Beyer Peacock, of Manchester; they were joined by six super-heated engines of the same wheel arrangement in 1913. So successful were they that the WAGR Midland workshops produced ten more, to a slightly modified design (Moa class), in 1930. Notable conventional locomotives were the F-class 4-8-0s (goods) and the E-class 4-6-2s (passenger) introduced in 1902; Baldwin Locomotive Works supplied thirty-two locomotives, twenty of them compounds, in 1901-2. The 4-6-2 wheel arrangement was favoured for main-line engines up to and after the Second World War, largely stemming from the P-class supplied initially by North British Locomotive Works in 1924.

In 1937 Western Australia was the first State to introduce diesel-electric railcars to Australia. Although quite successful, they were gradually replaced in common with most mixed and passenger services by a fleet of railway-owned buses from 1945. Today, country passenger services in WA are minimal. The diesel-electric locomotive was introduced to the WAGR with an order for eighteen 400hp shunters from BTH, England, closely followed by forty-eight X-class 1,100hp 2-Do-2 units from Metropolitan-Vickers, England. More recently, GM, English Electric and Alco-design MLW units have helped to complete dieselisation.

The State has benefited greatly from the construction of a 4ft 8½in-gauge line between Kalgoorlie and Perth. Subsequently, all former 3ft 6in gauge trackage east of Merredin, Western Australia, has been converted to 4ft 8½in, largely to cater for mineral traffic in the revitalised Leonora-Kalgoorlie-Esperance areas. Since 1965, there have been tremendous developments in iron ore-carrying privately owned railways in the north-west of the State. Four separate companies operate over 500 miles of heavy-duty 4ft 8½in track between mine sites and coastal ports, and another 200 miles were under construction in 1972. Diesel-electric 3,600hp locomotives in multiple haul 16,000-ton trains, a level of operation unknown elsewhere in Australia.

The federation of the six Australian States into the Commonwealth of Australia in 1901 brought with it a promise that east and west Australia would be linked by rail. Subsequent agreements between the Commonwealth and South Australian Governments brought about the transfer of the North Australia Railway and the Central Australia Railway to Commonwealth control and formation of the Commonwealth Railways as a separate entity. In 1911, an Act authorised construction of a 1,051-mile 4ft 8½in-gauge line from Port Augusta, South Australia, to Kalgoorlie, Western Australia. Active construction started in 1911 and, despite the treeless Nullarbor plain which the line crossed, it was completed in 1917.

When first acquired by the Commonwealth in 1911, the Palmerston (Darwin) to Pine Creek railway was administered by the Northern Territory Administration. It became part of Commonwealth Railways in 1918 and was extended as far south as Birdum by 1929.

The line from Port Augusta to Oodnadatta, also acquired by the Commonwealth in 1911, was leased back to South Australia for operation by the state system. Prior to an extension north to Alice Springs, Commonwealth Railways took over full operation in 1926. Alice Springs was reached in 1929, but throughout its life the line has suffered continually from floods. In 1976 construction began on a new 4ft 8½in gauge track to link Alice Springs with Tarcoola on the east-west line, and delays due to weather will be much reduced. Earlier, to cater for heavy coal traffic from Leigh Creek in South Australia, a new line of 4ft 8½in gauge was built on quite a different route from Port Augusta to Marree in 1957. The old line has now been abandoned except for the scenic Pichi Richi Pass section from Quorn which is operated as a tourist railway.

Problems of gauge differences were foreseen even before the first meeting of two systems of different gauge (at Albury in 1883). One notable step to reduce the problem took place in 1930 when a 4ft 8½in-gauge line from Grafton NSW to Brisbane was opened, obviating the need for transhipment at Wallangarra. Then, in 1937 Commonwealth Railways extended its 4ft 8½in-gauge line southwards from Port Augusta to Port Pirie, there to meet a new 5ft 3in-gauge line built from Red Hill, which was already connected to Adelaide; thus one other transhipment was eliminated. Finally, as a result of a Commonwealth Government committee report of 1956, three major traffic routes have been constructed or reconstructed. They are:

Albury (Wodonga, Victoria) to Melbourne — a new 4ft 8½in line running parallel to the existing 5ft 3in track, opened for traffic in January 1962.

Kalgoorlie to Fremantle and Perth — a

new 4ft 8½in 450-mile line, deviating from the former 3ft 6in route at the ends, opened throughout in 1968.

Broken Hill to Port Pirie – a 4ft 8½in line, largely parallel to the 3ft 6in line, opened at the beginning of 1970 to complete a trans-continental route of one gauge. Linked projects were upgrading work on the Parkes-Broken Hill line of the NSWGR and further rehabilitation on the Trans-Australian line.

Early in the 1970s the various systems joined public relations forces under the name 'Railways of Australia', and this

has promoted an impression of unity. Jointly-owned passenger rolling-stock designated 'Railways of Australia' is in service between Sydney and Perth on the *Indian Pacific* express, and container equipment styled 'Railways of Australia Container Express' (RACE) is widely in use.

The future of Australian railways, in the role of freight carriers, certainly looks bright; and it seems that, with long-distance passenger services continuing in many areas, a successful future is assured.

1. Pacific No 3809 on a mail train for Brisbane at Hawkesbury in March 1957. The bridge over the Hawkesbury river is 2,900ft long and was built about 90 years ago to complete the important East Coast route between Sydney, Newcastle and Brisbane. (*D. Cross*)

2. NSWGR passenger train at Wagga Wagga headed by a class-30 4-6-0. These engines were built from 1903 as 4-6-4 tank locomotives for Sydney suburban work but were rebuilt as tender locomotives when the local services were electrified. (*D. Cross*)

1

2

3

4

1. ÖBB 5,400hp Co-Co electric locomotive No 1110.17 leaving Innsbruck with SBB (Swiss) Vienna-Basle express train in August 1964. (*B. Stephenson*)

2 and 4. In June 1958 the Austrian Federal Railways (ÖBB) placed in service a luxury electric push-pull train for the Transalpin service between Vienna and Zurich (later Basle) in Switzerland. The train has been more than successful and in recent years has been run in two parts or with two train sets coupled together. From 1978 the train has been locomotive hauled, with new standard European coaches of both first and second class – unusual for European luxury trains which are normally first class only. In 2, one of the ÖBB Transalpin trains built in 1965 is seen near St Anton, and in 4 at Pöchlarn. (2, *Austrian Federal Railways*; 4, *J. R. Batts*)

3. Locomotive No 3, 'Tirol', of the Zillertalbahn at Mayrhofen in Austria, a line which still has steam locomotives as a tourist attraction. (*J. L. Champion*)

1. Achenseebahn's No 1 locomotive, built in 1889, at Maurach on one of Austria's narrow-gauge tourist steam lines which includes a rack-and-pinion section. (*J. L. Champion*)

2. A class-77 tank engine and local train on the Summerau line in 1971. With one or two exceptions, steam is almost a thing of the past in Austria, (*J. Winkley*)

3. ÖBB 760mm-gauge diesel locomotive No 2095.04 near Egg with a Bregenz-Bezau train in June 1967. (*B. Stephenson*)

4. No 97.208 banking a train of iron-ore empties on the climb out of Vordenberg in June 1969. This line, remarkable for being a standard-gauge branch but with a rack section, was built for carrying ore from the workings in the mountains but also has passenger trains. Diesel locomotives began trials on the line in 1978. (*B. Stephenson*)

5. An 0-8-4T engine, No 399.04, on one of the ÖBB's narrow-gauge lines at Gmund, near the Czechoslovak border. (*C. J. Gammell*)

2

3

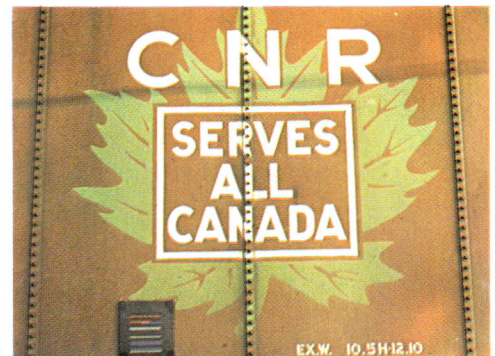

4

1. CP Rail's trans-continental train, 'The Canadian' of the 1960s, approaching Lake Louise, near Banff, with the Rockies in the background. CP Rail in the last decade has virtually opted out of the long-distance passenger business. (*CP Rail*)

2. Aerial shot of CN's 'SuperContinental' in the Jasper area. This train was CN's answer to CP's 'The Canadian' trans-Canada service but did not have the dome observation cars of the CP route. (*Canadian National Railways*)

3. On CP in 1959, Pacific No 2470 leaving Montreal Windsor Street station. (*J. N. Westwood*)

4. Early slogan of Canadian National Railways on the side of a boxcar. In 1978, surviving passenger services of both CP Rail and CNR were taken over by a new organisation called VIARail Canada, to change the image of once-famous railway names. (*J. R. Batts*)

1

2

▼ 3

1. A CPR 'Dayliner' diesel railcar at Kentville, Nova Scotia, on the CP subsidiary Dominion Atlantic Railway in September 1972. These stainless-steel railcars operate many of the surviving cross-country and local services in Canada and also in the United States. (*J. G. Tawse*)

2. CNR 4-8-4 No 6218, the last locomotive to work in steam in Canada in the late 1960s. (*P. B. Whitehouse*)

3. CP No 2317 of a standard 4-6-2 type introduced in the early 1920s and built over a long period. (*P. B. Whitehouse*)

4. Heading a freight train at Portland, Maine – CNR 2-8-2 No 3709. (*J. M. Jarvis*)

5. Pacific Great Eastern northbound passenger and southbound logging trains pass at mountain halt. This line, called the British Columbia Railway since 1972, operates more than 1,000 miles of route north from Vancouver. (*V. Goldberg*)

Overleaf: CNR's 'SuperContinental'. This is one of the last great transcontinental expresses running across North America, from Toronto and Montreal to Vancouver via Winnipeg and the Jasper National Park. Mount Robson, 12,972ft, is in the background. (*Canadian National Railways*

4

5

1. SAR class-24 2-8-4 near Aprilskraal on the Jamestown branch in July 1972. These engines, of which 100 were built by the North British Loco Co, were constructed especially for lightly laid branch lines and were introduced in 1948. (*J. Hunt*)

2. A Garratt taking water on the Umtata branch in eastern Cape Province in July 1972. Although new diesel locomotives and further main-line electrification have been commissioned in the 1970s, South Africa had more than 1,700 steam locomotives in service in 1978 which were not expected to be phased out until 1990. (*J. Hunt*)

3. SAR electric express passenger train on the Indian Ocean coast near Durban. (*By courtesy of South African Railways*)

4. Class-NG15 2ft-gauge locomotive wearing a diamond jubilee plaque of the South African Historic Transport Association on the Port Elizabeth-Avontur line at van Staden bridge in 1970. (*By courtesy of South African Railways*)

3

1. SAR class-198 4-8-2 climbing the Lootsberg pass, near Middelburg, in August 1967. This class of 14 locomotives was built in 1930 by Schwartzkopff Co of Berlin and intended for mixed-traffic duties on branch and cross-country lines. (*D. Huntriss*)

2. Normally used as a shed pilot, a SAR class-10C 4-6-2 on a Bloemfontein local train in October 1969. (*J. B. Snell*)

3. SAR 'Blue Train' on the electrified section between Cape Town and Beaufort West. The train is depicted here in the late 1960s, but in 1972 new sets of coaches were built specially for this luxury service with full air-conditioning, private bedrooms, showers and suites, besides more compact compartments.

4. The last serving SAR 6J 4-6-0 and a class-8 4-8-0 on a Bethlehem-Frankfort goods train in September 1969. (*J. B. Snell*)

4

1. Austrian-built (SGP) diesel locomotive on the Sofia-Pernick line in Bulgaria. (*C. J. Gammell*)

2. Russian class-E 0-10-0, built from 1912 onwards to become the world's largest class of over 13,000 engines. Russian railways operate mostly on the 5ft gauge; locomotives are the widest and tallest in the world, reaching almost 17ft high. (*C. J. Gammell*)

3. Czechoslovak State Railways' 4-8-2 No 498 112 at Zdice in April 1972. Steam is still well in evidence in Czechoslovakia although modern traction is gradually taking over on many routes. (*C. J. Gammell*)

4. Polish State Railways' type SM42 diesel locomotive at Poznan in June 1967. Although built for freight duties it is finished in an attractive green and yellow livery. (*C. K. Hemphill*)

4

1. Czechoslovak State Railways' standard 475.1-class mixed-traffic 4-8-2 crosses the Vltava river from Prague main station in October 1967. (*C. J. Gammell*)

2. USSR class-VL60 Co-Co 4,160kW 25kV electric locomotive with passenger train at Ulan Ude, east Siberia in November 1971. (*J. Holwell*)

3. Unofficial double-deck commuter train of Romanian State Railways (CFR) in the Bucharest rush hour. Electrification on the overhead system has stopped this joy-riding practice, but the CFR has in recent years introduced proper double-deck coaches on some commuter services. A feature of many of eastern European railways is the building of equipment in one country for use in another – even sometimes western European designs built under licence, for example Swiss- and Swedish-type locomotives built in Romania. (*L. King*)

Yugoslavia

It is probably true to say that, to the outside world, Yugoslavia has undergone a remarkable change during the past fifty years. Prior to the Second World War it was a new State with a young ex-Serbian king who had been to school in England; after the holocaust its resurgence as an uncommitted socialist republic, established at great cost under the leadership of Marshall Tito, made, to say the least, considerable impact both in the East and West. Now its coastline, mountains and

forests are open to, and a haven for, tourists of all nationalities, who are rarely disappointed.

Of all the centres, perhaps Dubrovnik is the best known, and Dubrovnik has not yet been spoilt. It sits at the foot of steep hills in a setting of great natural beauty. The coastal belt and nearby islands are covered in thick green vegetation, of pine woods, tropical plants, palms and cacti. Bougainvillea, oleander and many more colourful flowering trees and shrubs

Yugoslavia at one time had a large narrow-gauge mileage, in recent years closed or gradually replaced by new standard-gauge routes. Class-83 0-8-2s worked the 760mm gauge line between Dubrovnik and Belgrade. (*R. A. H. Casling*)

abound, as well as fruit trees, olives and vines. But the foreground to this Riviera-like coast is a remarkable contrast to the hinterland of barren mountains, which stretch back to Sarajevo and back again, though greener, towards the north.

These days there are two main ways of reaching Dubrovnik, by crowded boat down the coast from Venice or Rijeka, cruising through the lovely Dalmatian islands, or by air to the small airfield with its flowered terrace and a partiality for charter flights and their package tours. But not so long ago, indeed within the last decade, one could have travelled overland by train taking the Orient Express to Belgrade and then by 760mm (2ft 6in) narrow-gauge train over the 425 miles via Sarajevo and crossing five mountain ranges with great spiral tunnels, and a rack section thrown in for good measure. The origin of the 760mm gauge, like so many other good things in life, was an accident; the contractors Hügel-Sager happened to have some primitive rolling stock of the gauge available, left over from their construction of the Temesvar-Orsova Railway in Romania.

The story of Yugoslav Railways as a whole is historically and currently interesting. Historically, the system has been inherited from the remnants of the old Austro-Hungarian Empire added to that of the old Kingdom of Serbia; currently, the country is one of the few in Europe to construct new lines to give better and faster services to the principal towns from the capital to the coast. Perhaps naturally, the once essential but slow narrow-gauge system has been affected by the new construction, which has now reached Posega from Belgrade and runs from Sarajevo to the coast at Ploce.

Most of the narrow-gauge lines in Yugoslavia were the result of the Austrian occupation of Bosnia, Herzegovina and Dalmatia in the 1870s, for that dominion could only be made effective by improvement of communications. One of the first tasks was to build a railway from the Sava to the Adriatic coast – in fact from Belgrade to Dubrovnik. The northern section, including the spiral tunnels between Uzice and Visegrad, reached Sarajevo in 1884 and the southern part got as far as Mostar by 1885. It was the middle section which proved to be the most difficult, for it involved a rise to a summit level of 2,800 feet, with several sections as steeply graded as 1 in 16 that had to be worked by rack and pinion; the section was not completed until 1890. The whole system was worked by the military authorities until 1895. Of the whole line from Belgrade to Dubrovnik only about twenty-four per cent was level track.

Trains ran through from Belgrade to Sarajevo, and from Sarajevo to Dubrovnik until comparatively recently but during the last decade change has been the order of the day, and in particular the coming of the new standard-gauge line. From Sarajevo the new railway takes one to Capljina. From there on the narrow gauge runs over the bleak and heat-shimmering hills via Hutovo and Hum down the spirals to the blue Adriatic and trains are

diesel multiple units for passengers.

But it is not long back since the mighty Orient Express, with its blue Wagons-Lits sleeping cars, running on to places farther east – Dimitrovgrad, Sofia and Istanbul or perhaps Athens – met the diminutive trains, which had backed quietly into the main terminus in Belgrade. The locomotive, probably built in Budapest, would be liberally sprinkled with domes and sandboxes, and the dark and somewhat ancient coaches would be filled with a noisy throng of passengers waiting to return to the countryside, the women in trousers and headcloths and the men in breeches and long black stockings or long tight trousers like jodhpurs.

The coaches, through to Sarajevo, would take over twelve hours for the journey, and would include first-class as well as slatted-seat second-class accommodation and possibly a buffet car. Engines would most likely be changed at Titovo Uzice or Visegrad, where the last and heaviest of the gruelling climbs along the sides of gorges and though numerous tunnels begins. The first four to five hours of the journey was over undulating countryside, but gradually climbing up to Cacak and on to Titovo Uzice – the headquarters of Marshall Tito and his Partisans for a short period in the Second World War, when they declared the first Independent Yugoslav Republic. There were a small engine-shed and repair shops at Titovo Uzice and locomotives on through trains were sometimes changed there.

From its starting point at Titovo Uzice, the railway climbed up along and above the river through a mile-long tunnel at the summit, before dropping by spirals through more tunnels and alongside the road, to reach Visegrad about three hours later. The line then climbed up along the Driva gorge to the little junction station of Ustipraca, and on up into the forest and bear country of Praca, before winding down the wooded mountainside to the environs of Sarajevo and into the Alipasin Most station after a journey time of about four hours.

Until the coming of the new standard-gauge line the narrow-gauge train ran into a remote corner of Sarajevo Novo station, to and from which the southern section trains and those to Belgrade also ran. The climb up to the summit at Ivan, about thirty miles out of Sarajevo, was later altered to ease the next section, which was the 1 in 16 descent to Konjic. A post-war re-alignment bypassed the old line by means of a two-mile tunnel ending at Bradina station. The section from Bradina to Konjic, a distance of six and a half miles, was rack operated. The northbound (uphill) traffic on the section was dense, for trains were slow anyway on the abnormal gradient and long trains needed to be split and worked up in sections. In additions, all northbound steam trains had to stop at Brotani pod Ivanom for water. Altogether, the time for the six-and-a-half-mile journey was one

hour fifteen minutes, including locomotive changes, and if the train had to be split it took about one hour forty-five minutes. (Diesel multiple-unit trains, which were not rack fitted, took forty-five minutes.)

The Bradina-Konjic section was wild and wooded; during the war it was fine guerilla country and the scene of a great deal of hard fighting against the Germans. In *Disputed Barricades*, Sir Fitzroy Maclean (Lord Ballantrae) describes the havoc wrought by a partisan raid on Bradina station when an enemy garrison was taken by surprise. Before leaving, they dynamited the bridge, blocked the tunnel and sent a train of thirty-three wagons down the grade and over a precipice into the Neretva river. It was over 125 miles from Konjic to Dubrovnik and the line followed the Neretva valley all the way, via Jablanica to the Moslem town of Mostar, another engine-changing point.

Mostar is set against a background of mosques and mountains, and in narrow-gauge days the shed there was full of 0-8-2s of the 83 class and 2-8-2s of the 85 class, with white wheel rims, highly polished brasswork and even shining shell-cases full of flowers on the running plates. Leaving Mostar, the line followed the broadening Neretva vally to Gabela, where the way became more mountainous and the climb up to Hutovo began. Capljina, situated just before the climb proper begins, is the terminus of the southern-section narrow-gauge today.

Once again the line climbs high up into the hills, the scenery becoming wilder and bleaker and the curves more tortuous, to the watershed of the rivers Neretva and Trebisnica. As the grade steepens the rails lead into high plateau country, bare in the extreme. There the labouring steam engines (double-headed for the climb) heaved their ten or eleven coaches, running to about 125 tons, round horse-shoe curves, with flanges squealing and eldritch whistles shrieking; despite the huge spark arresters fitted to the engines, they provided a tremendous display of pyrotechnics after dark. The line passes the tiny junction of Hum, where the Titograd line once branched off, and continues downhill to Dubrovnik through more spiral tunnels and loops.

For many years the main motive power on the Sava-Adriatic sections consisted of three classes of normal adhesion engines and one class of rack engine. The former included the sprightly 73-class 2-6-2s built by Krauss between 1907 and 1913, which gave good service for over fifty years and only began to disappear as traffic was transferred elsewhere; there were also 83-class 0-8-2s and the 85-class 2-8-2s. Until the completion of the standard-gauge line to Sarajevo after the last war, other magnificent machines were to be seen. There were 2-6-6-0 Mallets which hauled the heavy freights over the high mountains from Visegrad eastwards; where necessary they were banked by a class of 2-6-6-0 Mallet tanks. Sadly, the completion of the standard-gauge line robbed the section of much of its freight and the Mallets were scrapped.

The motive power on the 760mm gauge comprised two classes of steam engines, some new diesel locomotives and some very comfortable modern rail-car sets. Most numerous steamers were of the 83 class, already mentioned, the first of which were built by Krauss between 1903 on 1908. Later batches were built by Jung between 1923 and 1934 and further additions came from Budapest in 1929. After a gap of nearly twenty years another thirty were constructed by the Yugoslavs at Slavonski Brod in 1948-49. The second type regularly at work on this section was the 85-class 2-8-2s built at Budapest in 1930; they have superheaters and piston valves and became the standard heavy-duty mixed-traffic engines. The last batch of Class 85s was also built at Slavonksi Brod after the war.

Two other classes in regular use until recently were the UNRRA 0-8-0s built by Porter in America and shipped to Yugoslavia under lend-lease, and the rack 0-6-4s of the 97 class used on the Bradina-Konjic section, built at Florisdorf in 1894. The Yugoslav Railways had a number of the Class 97 engines, which were interesting for having independent sets of cylinders and motion for the adhesion and rack drives, and for needing considerable driving skill! Each engine had two regulators and two sets of reversing gear; keeping them in unison was a difficult task ordinarily and even more so when double-headed as the leading engine emerged onto normal track after leaving the rack.

Today this once huge system is truncated and its future is tied up with the final construction targets of the new standard-gauge lines. Trains still run through Capljina to Dubrovnik and are almost entirely diesel multiple units. Steam, in the form of the 83 class and a few 85 class, very occasionally works the freights. There are also said to be occasional locals going part of the way which are steam hauled. But steam or diesel, the journey must be one of the finest and most dramatic in Europe and tailor-made for tourists looking for something out of the ordinary on their holidays.

It is to be hoped that the Dubrovnik to Hum line might, one day, be used for tourist steam; at any rate a scheme has been put forward as a possibility. There is little doubt that it, like so many other European tourist steam lines, would be a sell-out; and what a journey it would be!

1. **Pacific 05.028 heading the famous 'Orient Express' at Crveni Krst in October 1968.** (*C. J. Gammell*)

2. **Much-used 0-4-0T of the 60cm-gauge Ohrid Railway in south Montenegro, Yugoslavia, in 1962.** (*F. L. Pugh*)

3. **Class-85 No 85.005 on a mixed train makes a stop at Bioska in October 1958. Regrettably, closures of parts of the 760mm-gauge network and the introduction of diesel traction on most passenger services in recent years mean that these 2-8-2s have little other work than occasional freights.** (*C. J. Gammell*)

1. East German Pacific No 01 525 on a cross-border express near Honebach, West Germany, in June 1968. With the end of steam traction in West Germany in 1977, through workings by East German steam locomotives on cross-border trains, which had ceased a few years earlier, were but a memory. Steam locomotives live on in the Democratic Republic and Pacifics such as those shown on these two pages still handle certain express passenger trains. (*C. J. Gammell*)

2. DR rebuilt class-52.8 with Giesl ejector (left) and unrebuilt class-52 at Stendal shed in April 1972. The basic class-52 2-10-0 in its varied forms was built in large numbers during and after the Second World War and could be found at work in several European countries. Indeed, it was the second most numerous type ever built, with more than 6,000 engines, nearly all constructed between 1942 and 1945. (*B. Stephenson*)

3. East German (DR) Pacific No 03 180 leaving Hamburg for Berlin in April 1968. (*R. Bastin*)

03 180

1. DR Russian-built V200 Co-Co diesel-electric and V100 B-B diesel-hydraulic of domestic build heading a freight train of tank wagons out of Hof for East Germany in May 1969. (*B. Stephenson*)

2. DR (East German) diesel-hydraulic motor train leaving Prague on the Vindabone Vienna-Berlin service in June 1969. (*B. Stephenson*)

1. French experimental gas turbo-electric advanced passenger train's first appearance at Belfort in April 1972. After the success of earlier gas-turbine trains this unit was developed for trials in high-speed running at up to 180mph. (*La Vie du Rail: Y. Broncard*)

2. Following the introduction of the gas-turbine trains running at top speeds of 110mph between Paris and Caen in 1970, French Railways (SNCF) ordered higher-power RTG turbotrains for cross-country services designed for maximum speeds of 125mph. (*SNCF*)

3. Large autorail and trailers on a rural section of the Côtes du Nord Railway, one of the many French narrow-gauge secondary lines, virtually none of which now exists. Two or three have been restored as tourist lines with steam traction. (*Colourviews Ltd*)

4

1. The Vivarais narrow-gauge system, south of Lyons, at one time extended over 120 miles through the mountains west of the Rhône Valley but was closed in 1968, when this picture of one of the line's 0-6-6-0 Mallet tanks was taken. (*C. J. Gammell*)

2. An old two-class double-deck coach of the French Est Railway network in pre-SNCF days. (*Jean-Claude Roca*)

3. Ex-Nord compound Pacific 231E23 at Calais Maritime in October 1966. These engines worked the principal expresses in northern France for more than 30 years until electrification. (*J. M. Cramp*)

4. A pair of SNCF diesel railcars in June 1967. SNCF uses diesel railcars on many branch, cross-country and local services. (*B. Stephenson*)

5. 141TC 2-8-2 tank locomotives on push-pull trains at Paris Gare du Nord. Many local trains are still worked by push-pull electric locomotives. (*C. M. Whitehouse*)

6. Diesel railcars of the Réseau du Tarn at Castres in April 1960. (*F. L. Pugh*)

5

6

China

In writing about the railways of China a difficulty is that there are no official figures to use as a basis. Nevertheless, a picture emerges of a railway system with some 25,000 miles of route — more than twice that of Britain. It carries four times as much freight and one-third the number of passengers. However, the Chinese National Railways serve a population more than ten times larger and an area ten times bigger; this explains why they have grown fourfold from the 6,000 usable miles that existed when the Mao regime took over in 1949 and are still growing. Lines now penetrate far into the Chinese parts of central Asia; in particular, there is a line to Uranchi in Sinkiang Province, the far north-western corner of China. Tibet, however, has still to be penetrated by rail — but, if present plans mature, it soon will be.

From the spectator's point of view, the main lines in the parts of China accessible to Western tourists look like American 'standard railroading' of the Second World War, with freight trains hauled by steam (and an occasional diesel) and passenger trains by diesel with occasionally steam. The illusion of being in the USA with the clock put back is almost complete as great trains of buck-eye-coupled bogie cars go roaring by behind big black 2-10-2s. Left-hand running and raised station platforms, which come easily to a British eye, are the principal non-American features.

During Mao Tse-Tung's 'Great Leap Forward' of 1958 to 1960, the Chinese Railways had some traumatic experience with do-it-yourself diesel locomotives and their premature large-scale production, so it is not surprising that they then set out to build the world's last steam locomotive factory at Tatung (northwest of Pekin) besides continuing steam production elsewhere. Although reliable diesel locomotives are now coming off Chinese production lines at the estimated rate of 200 a year, steam locomotives are apparently also still being built on a reduced scale. It is thought that the diesel fleet is currently between 1,000 and 2,000 and that there are approximately 5,000 steam locomotives, of which rather more than half are Chinese built. Electrification is at present on a small scale, far away in the mountains of central China.

Reports that new steam locomotives were still being built in China were hard to believe back in Europe, but the writer and illustrators of this article actually stood on the station platform at the tragic town of Tangshan, three short weeks before it was destroyed in the

Steam at Tangshan: JF-class 2-8-2 locomotives on duty marshalling coal trains. (*Colourviews Publications: C. M. Whitehouse*)

1

earthquake of 28 July 1976, looking at a row of brand-new consecutively numbered little 2-8-2s. They had just been completed in the locomotive works there. No objection was made to our taking pictures, in fact we were encouraged to do so. Steam construction has now ceased at Tangshan, but apparently continues elsewhere.

It is not easy for a lover of steam to visit this far-away land. Firstly because the Chinese admit only few organised tourist groups to their country and, for these, there are long waiting lists. Secondly, they find it difficult to understand even the concept of railway enthusiasm — the first two parties of railway lovers (one Australian and one British) found their programme inclined towards a look at Chinese life in general rather than railways in particular. In the case of the British group, on only ten days out of the twenty spent in China was there more than a glimpse of railways, but when an official visit or journey did take place the rewards were great. In fact, two out of the six train journeys were behind steam and over 300 steam locomotives were observed and recorded. Steam still rules, OK!

One must add, though, that, once

2

permission to enter has been granted, and the traveller reaches the frontier, reception is delightful. Dover and Folkestone have a great deal to learn from a country that provides armchairs and a free delicious lunch in the course of its Customs Immigration formalities, but that is what happens on entering China via the railway from British Kowloon (Hong Kong) to Canton. The cleanliness, consideration and courtesy encountered on arrival is in fact typical of the way tourists are treated there.

Both the Chinese and British sections of the Kowloon-Canton Railway are completely dieselised, but everywhere else that the two groups of tourists went there was not only steam but new steam

1. Diesel No 0115 enters Pekin station with a train from Shanghai to Tientsin, Tangshan and the north. (*Colourviews Publications: P. B. Whitehouse*)

2. Hard-class passengers freshening up after the night's journey en route from Tientsin to Shanghai. (*Colourviews Publications: P. B. Whitehouse*)

3. Two modern Chinese diesel locomotives Nos 0035 and 2066 waiting their turn of duty at Pekin station. (*Colourviews Publications: C. M. Whitehouse*)

(mostly built since the rest of the world — with the exception of India — ceased to make steam locomotives) maintained, moreover, in excellent condition. Of the types seen by the two tours, which covered a mere twentieth of the system but included what seem likely to be the steamiest main lines in the east of the country, pride of place must go to the magnificent standard 2-10-2 *Qian Jing* (March Forward) or QJ class. The QJs are very much in the American tradition but based directly on the Russian LV class and have 5ft 0in diameter driving wheels and a nominal top speed of 50mph, a speed at which they seem very much at home with 2,500 tons or so behind the drawbar. The axle load is 20 tons and the total weight in working order, including an eight-wheel tender, 149 tons. A version with a twelve-wheel tender also exists for working on lines where the distance between water plugs is long. Construction started at Dairen (Dalny) under Russian guidance on a small scale in 1956, but full production had to wait until the breach between the two countries had been resolved and the completion of the Tatung Works, which was specially laid out for large-scale QJ building. Since these visits, another visitor who was taken to Tatung has reported that the QJ is still being made there. With new policies being adopted following the death of Chairman Mao, it does not seem likely that this will carry on for long.

A feature of Chinese Railways is the height of the loading gauge, which is the highest on any standard-gauge railway in the world (except for one just completed in Gabon). In the QJ design advantage is taken of this to run the main steam-pipe in a big insulated casing along the top of the boiler forward from the dome to a regulator box just behind the chimney. This arrangement is very noticeable in the illustrations. The high loading gauge made it possible to find a home for surplus Russian steam power when, as a stopgap, a large number of Russian FD class 1-5-1s (believed to be as many as 2,000) were obtained. These locomotives, built during the decade 1931-41, had become surplus in their native land due to the encroachment of electrification and dieselisation on the lines to which they were confined because of their 20-ton axle load. After gauge conversion from 5ft 0in to 4ft 8½in, the Chinese Railways have found them useful machines, although their original name *Friendship* is no longer appropriate — in China they are now just plain FD. Many examples were seen in the Nanking and Shanghai areas in the south-east of the country; the irreverent British group christened them Flying Donkeys, to the great delight of their Chinese railway hosts, who felt it was at least a token riposte to the humiliations the Chinese received at the hands of the Russians.

Lesser freight workings, such as local trips and shunting, are mainly in the hands of a variety of 2-8-2s of three main types, of which several sub-groups could be recognised. The *Jie Fang* (Liberation), or JF, is of pure American lineage and, indeed, early examples were seen still with USA builders' plates. On the other hand, the design of the *Jian She* (Construction) JS class is pure American but construction took place in Japan.

Both are similar in size with 53in diameter driving wheels and an all-up weight of 123 tons. The brand-new locomotives referred to earlier, which the party was shown at Tangshan, were slightly smaller (though by how much it was impossible to quantify) and known as the *Shang You* (Aiming High) or SY class.

During the British party's trip by bus to visit a farming commune in the Tangshan area, the road taken lay parallel to a branch line, of which the bridges bore the date 1971. Two mixed trains and a freight seen here were all SY hauled, presenting the remarkable spectacle of 1970s steam locomotives working a 1970s branch line.

On local freight and shunting duties in the Shanghai and Canton areas some USA-built 2-8-0s are to be seen. They

Pacifics seen had them merely stencilled on; in fact, the details of the decor in all locomotives seen showed considerable variations on the basic pattern; obviously different depots (and possibly even individual drivers) had freedom to embellish as they pleased. Patriotic slogans were very common.

Of other passenger power, there was just a glimpse of one example of an older class of Pacific with the same size

1. Steam power in the 1970s: QJ-class 2-10-2 at Tientsin. (*J. B. Hollingsworth*)

2. UNRAA power: KD-class 2-8-0, built in the USA, at Shanghai. (*J. B. Hollingsworth*)

were originally supplied to the Kuomintang regime under the auspices of the United Nations in quite large numbers during 1946-47. The United Nations also sent over some ex-Great Western Railway 0-6-0 'Dean Goods' locomotives – they were ones that had spent the war on the continent of Europe – but, perhaps not surprisingly, no trace of them was seen.

Apart from occasional local working, all the steam passenger trains encountered were hauled by *Ren Ming* (People's) RM class Pacifics, with 5ft 9in diameter wheels and a maximum speed of 70mph which they were able to maintain for long periods with heavy trains of fourteen 45-ton cars. As on the QJs, the external main steam-pipe casing forward of the dome is a notable feature. Some RM Pacifics, in addition to the usual red wheels, white tyres and vermilion buffer beams which relieve the black of the rest, had all their insignia, both lettering and numbering, in polished brass. This was by no means usual and other

cylinders and wheels, the *Sheng Li* (Victory), but none of the great British-built 4-8-4s, built by the Vulcan Foundry for the Shanghai-Nanking Railway in 1937; they were, however, working as late as 1966 as class KF. A recent illustration has appeared in the west of a big-wheeled passenger similar to the Russian Josef Stalin class, in use in China; and also one of a streamlined 4-6-2, one of those supplied by Japan for working the high-speed *Asia Express* in Manchuria before the war.

The passenger trains of the Chinese Railways have a good deal to commend them. The Soft-class sleeping cars are similar to the European first-class couchette, but kept spotlessly clean. At the modest speeds run, the riding is excellent and the catering in the dining-car very much in the Chinese tradition: simple, fresh and good. Air-conditioning was noted only on the prestige run from the Hong Kong frontier to Canton. Hard-class cars, of which there are both the couchette

and the open sitting variety, are plain but also clean. The only feature towards which the Westerner might direct caution is hole-in-the-floor lavatories.

The world's railways are divided into those with open stations as, for example, in Switzerland and those with closed, as in Britain. The Chinese come very definitely into the latter category. Yet, they have never heard of a platform ticket. Adequate waiting-rooms are provided in which goodbyes can be said, so, the Chinese would argue, where is the need for platform tickets. Foreigners, and, one suspects natives also, cannot buy even a short-distance travel ticket without a permit, so there is no way to gain access to a station platform without special arrangement.

Pekin's magnificent main station was built in 1959 as part of the 'Great Leap Forward'. Construction, including all the design and planning, took less than a year. There are six platforms with twelve faces and, although it is a terminus, the

main building is set at the side rather than the end, with the concourse at first-floor level above the platform. Waiting-rooms, provided for each main direction of travel, are not only clean and comfortable but almost luxurious. There are very fine dining-rooms, nurseries and other amenities. The main signal-box is a room off one of the administrative corridors in the top floor of the block and above that there is a noble clock tower with a pagoda roof, which chimes 'The East is Red' at noon, 3 and 6pm. There are fifty-eight departures daily. Subtracting seven local trains, one finds that barely more than fifty main-line trains serve a capital city of some four million inhabitants, who have no private cars, no long-distance buses and only minimal air services.

Signalling on the main line is mostly conventional multi-aspect colour light, but areas of semaphore do exist to match the traditional motive power. At first glance they appear to be of old-fashioned British lower quadrant pattern; closer scrutiny shows the arms to be of the American type but, because of the left-hand running, seen as if in a looking-glass. Still deeper examination gives the impression that, when several arms are mounted on the same post, the aspects displayed and their meanings owe something to German inspiration. To complete the international picture, it may be added that in the old days the whistle boards on the Pekin-Hankow Railway bore the French legend *Sifflez*!: all of which reflects the piecemeal way in which the Chinese railway system was developed before the First World War by different foreign powers.

Current Chinese practice in regard to the permanent way again follows world-wide convention with long welded rail and concrete sleepers, but much steam-age track also exists, generally in the American tradition. Six-bolt fishplates are the rule and enable the traveller departing from China as he walks across the railway bridge at Low Wu to detect the last Communist rail and the first Imperial one. Most British visitors feel some regret at leaving, mainly because it means saying goodbye to guides who have become firm friends, but they would probably also admit to a certain easing of the mind when, once more, they enter a building flying the Union Jack.

In the long term, of course, steam traction has no future in China, but a greatly expanded railway system does. The Railway Technical Institute at Tientsin trains over 150 Railway Graduate Engineers each year and their work is gradually and literally leaving its mark in tremendous but little-known projects in the mountainous regions of western China. If present plans come to fruition, there is little doubt that it will not be long before the *Tibet Limited* pulls out of an enlarged Pekin station on its journey to the still forbidden city of Lhasa, crossing summits exceeding those of South America in the process.

1. One of the most spectacular railways in India is the 2ft-gauge Darjeeling-Himalaya Railway, originally built to serve the hill station at Darjeeling. Its tiny, over-worked 0-4-0 saddle tanks fairly blast their way up 1 in 20 gradients with sharp curves and spirals to climb into the mountains. (*E. Talbot*)

2. Turning W-class 0-6-2 No 569 on the 2ft 6in-gauge line at Nadiad. (*L. G. Marshall*)

3. HPS-class 4-6-0 No 24262 on a local train at Futwah in November 1970. The HPS-class was one of the standard types evolved by British engineers and built for, or by, several Indian railways, with variations, from about 1915 until 1951. (*L. G. Marshall*)

4. Central Railway narrow-gauge class-ZA/5 2-8-4T (Hunslet 1959) at Mahari junction in February 1968. (*E. Talbot*)

5. Diesel-hauled passenger train on the narrow-gauge Matheran Steam Tram line in the Bombay Ghats. (*E. Talbot*)

Following spread: Indian Railways were still building new steam locomotives until the early 1970s. More than 500 of these standard 5ft 6in-gauge class-WP Pacifics were built from 1947 and they are still in main-line service. (*T. B. Owen*)

1. A 1926 Werkspoor 60cm-gauge 0-8-0T, No TD10.02, at Krawang, Java, in August 1970. (*T. B. Owen*)

2. Beyer Peacock tram engine of the early 1900s at work on Indonesian State Railways near Surabaya, Java, in August 1972. (*C. J. Gammell*)

3. Indonesia State Railways' 2-8-2T (built in Holland by Werkspoor, 1922) approaching Tjiandjur with a train from Pandalarang in Java in August 1970. (*T. B. Owen*)

1. Indonesian 2-6-6-0 articulated tank engine No CC10.04 at Pandalarang, Java, in August 1970. *(T. B. Owen)*

2. Indonesian State Railways' 2-4-0 No B5014, by Sharp Stewart in 1885, at Madiun shed in September 1970. Steam was well in evidence in Indonesia in the 1970s and included many antiques such as this, but gradually diesels have been ousting these attractive veterans and some of the more recent steam types too. *(T. B. Owen)*

3. Awaiting a turn at Maos in August 1972: Indonesian State Railways' 0-4-0 No B5206. *(C. J. Gammell)*

4. The Indonesian numbering system for steam locomotives included a letter prefix denoting the number of driving-axles, A=1, B=2, C=3 etc. Here is 4-4-0 No B5308 near Madiun in Java (Ponogoro branch) in August 1972. *(C. J. Gammell)*

3

4

1. An Italian State Railways' diesel railcar near Crescentino in May 1972. (*L. King*)

2. A class-E646 Bo-Bo-Bo electric locomotive crossing the Adige river bridge as it leaves Verona with a train for Venice in 1967. Most Italian main lines are now electrified. (*B. Stephenson*)

3. Italian State Railways' track maintenance men at work at Ventimiglia near the Franco-Italian frontier. (*Italian State Railways*)

4. An express passenger electric multiple-unit train of class-Ale 601. (*Italian State Railways*)

5. Two 625-class 2-6-0 locomotives heading an evening train to Bassano out of Venice in September 1971. (*D. H. Wilson*)

Overleaf: Franco-Crosti 2-8-0 No 743 005 at Cava Carbonara in March 1970. The Franco-Crosti boiler includes a pre-heater unit in which exhaust gases pass through to heat feed-water before entering the boiler. (*L. King*)

5

1. Later type of Italian Ale 601 high-speed electric which in trials has reached speeds of 155mph. The aerials on the front are for direct signalbox to train communication to supplement normal lineside signalling. (*Italian State Railways*)

2. ETR220 electric mu train forming the Trieste-Genoa 'Rapido' at Brescia in October 1971. (*E. Tonarelli*)

Facing page:

1. Undoubtedly the world's greatest railway success of this century has been the building of new high-speed railways in Japan during the 1960s. Built to 4ft 8½in gauge instead of Japan's standard 3ft 6in gauge, the new lines carry exclusively high-speed electric trains running at 130-155mph.

Here a Tokyo-Osaka New Tokaido Line (NTL) train crosses one of the viaducts found to be necessary in constructing the high-speed line. (*Japanese Embassy, London*)

2. Although of different gauges. NTL and old lines are brought together at all stations on the new line. (*Japanese Embassy, London*)

🟥 Japan

1

2

1 and 2. Japan's large urban population calls for mass transportation around and across cities which is met by expanding networks of suburban and underground railways. Typical are these rapid-transit lines – a cross between a tram and conventional old-style railways – such as those depicted here of the Sapporo Rapid Transit System. Picture 1 is a train of the East-West line, and 2 shows a train on the South-North line. (*Sapporo Rapid Transit*)

3. An NTL train makes one of its infrequent station stops. Express passenger trains are formed of 12-coach, streamlined, electric multiple-unit stock. (*Picturepoint*)

1. One of the Dutch-Swiss diesel push-pull TEE sets on the Etoile du Nord service in 1960. These four-car first-class-only luxury trains operated various Trans-Europe Express services between Holland and Switzerland, and also in Belgium and France from 1957 until the early 1970s. All four trains were then sold to Canada and in 1977 were placed in service on the Ontario Northland Railway between Toronto and Kapuskasing (*E. S. Russell*)

2. Netherlands Railways (NS) class-1100 80-ton Bo-Bo of about 3,000hp built by the French firm Alstholm. The locomotive is shown here in its original livery of blue with stainless-steel bands. NS employs overhead electrification at 1,500volts direct current. (*B. Bond*)

3. Present-day view of Dutch 1100-class Bo-Bo locomotive, in blue and yellow livery with NS reversed arrow motif, at the head of International Sleeping Car Co (CIWLT) sleeping cars. (*Nederlandse Spoorwegen*)

4. Modern rail/tram/bus interchange station on Netherlands Railways. The tram acts as a feeder to long-distance rail services. The Inter City train in the background is hauled by NS 2,700hp Co-Co electric locomotive No 1501, one of a class of seven former British Railways' locomotives built for the Manchester-Sheffield line and sold to Holland. (*Nederlandse Spoorwegen*)

3

4

New Zealand

1. New Zealand Railways' express 'The Southerner', the South Island's crack train which runs daily the 369 miles between Christchurch and Invercargill, pictured at Dunedin. At the head is Japanese-built Dj Bo-Bo-Bo diesel No 1204, one of sixty-four locomotives which completed dieselisation of the South Island. (*D. B. Leitch*)

2. Blue Streak Express railcar at Taihape during a stop on the 426-mile journey between Auckland and Wellington. (*D. B. Leitch*)

3. Diesel railcar on a Greymouth-Christchurch service at Ofira gorge on the South Island. (*Colourviews: D. Cross*)

4. A class-Da GM diesel locomotive heading a summer-holiday scenic daylight express at Taihape. These 78-ton NZR AIA-AIA locomotives were built by General Motors in USA, Canada and Australasia and cover many North Island services. (*D. B. Leitch*)

Following spread: New Zealand Railways' Ja-class No 1267 on a delivery excursion to a steam museum at Frankton, near Rotorua, in North Island. The Ja 4-8-2 was the last steam class to be introduced by NZR from 1946 and was intended for South Islands service, although a British-built batch went to the North Island. Ja 4-8-2s lasted on the South Island until 1972. (*D. B. Leitch*)

3

1. An A-class Pacific, No 161, approaching Bluff with a goods train from Invercargill in March 1956. These engines were originally built as compounds in 1906 specifically for North Island main-line service, but they were rebuilt as simples from 1941 for more general duties. (*Colourviews: D. Cross*)

2. Ww-class engine No 571 heads an evening train across a bridge in spring 1970. This class dated from 1913 and were all-purpose 4-6-4 tank engines designed for branch and main-line stopping passenger trains and for freight. (*D. B. Leitch*)

3. A southbound goods train headed by a Ka 4-8-4 and an Aa Pacific signalled into a passenger loop as it climbs a slope on the Auckland-Wellington main line in winter 1954, with snow-covered volcanic Mts Ruapahu and (right) Ngarahoe behind. (*D. Cross*)

4. Class-AB Pacific No 720 heading a Christchurch-Picton goods train at Weka pass, Waikari, banked by another of the same class at the back, in January 1957. (*Colourviews: D. Cross*)

3

4

Portugal: The Narrow Gauge Lines

1

Without question the time to visit the narrow-gauge railways of Portugal is early autumn, for in late September and early October the vineyards in the precipitous valleys along which many of the railways run are busy with the harvest. Up along the Douro valley and its tributaries, the grapes ripen at much the same time and, as it once was with the hops of Kent and Sussex, there is seldom enough local labour to go round. So groups of harvesters and treaders, whole families, entire villages even, often of three generations, form teams of up to a hundred or so and go on their annual outings. Then the little metre-gauge trains chug along the vine-clad valley of the Corgo from Regua to Vila Real and up to Chaves, coaches packed to the roofs, with a magnificent range of sounds coming from the accordians, guitars, mouth-organs and drums.

In other seasons the valley railways are much quieter, and the traffic is more suitable to the diesel railcar which is beginning to throb along them; but steam is still there in abundance and many of the trains are mixed, with wagon-loads of grain or fruit, or metallic ores, trundling along with the passenger stock, and the ever-present dark-red postal van. Mostly the passengers are country folk off to market or a regular country fair, and children going to and from school. Most trains carry first-class and third-class stock, the former with seats protected by white linen covers and very clean, the latter with hard wooden slatted seats.

There are no dining-cars on the narrow-gauge lines, nor are there refreshment rooms except at the larger termini or junctions, though there is usually a wine-counter hidden away in most of the station buildings; they are not to be despised. Most of the passengers, be they locals, priests, returning emigrants, or members of the services, bring their own food — fish-cakes made with dried cod (*bolinhos de bacalhau*) or smoked ham from Chaves and delicious crusty bread, accompanied by wine in bottle, cask or leather wineskin. Most of the stations are inhabited by a water-seller during the summer months, for Portugal can be a very hot country then and the valleys can be particularly grilling.

1. **Portuguese Railways' (CP) Kessler-built 0-6-0T at Tua in September 1970.** (*C. J. Gammell*)

2. **Conversation piece in September 1971 at Tua station, on the narrow-gauge Tua-Braganca line. This line is one of the cluster of narrow-gauge railways leading off the Douro valley where steam has survived into the late 1970s, although not on all traffic. Many of the older locomotives have been withdrawn.** (*A. G. Orchard*)

These little lines serve some historic and attractive places up in the province of Tras os Montes (Behind the Mountains), such as the great fortress churches of the Sabor valley on the line close to the Spanish border. They have romantic names too — Mogadouro, Miranda do Douro, and Freizo de Espada a Cintra (the Ash of the Girt Sword), recalling the days of the border wars and the Moorish raids. Then there is Braganca, the railhead of the Tua line, another border town giving its name to the Royal House of Portugal and the Imperial House of Brazil.

There are three main groups of metre-

2

gauge lines, all in the north of the country. The first and easiest to visit is probably that based on the Porto Trindade station. From there, all trains run out over a steeply-graded section of double track to Senhora da Hora which is the junction for Vila do Conde and Povoa de Varzim in one direction, and Fafe in the other. This busy suburban service is now converted to diesel working. Moving eastwards, there are the picturesque lines (each completely separate and unconnected with any other narrow-gauge system) along the Douro Valley. Going east from Porto they are the Tamega line (Livracao to Amarante and Arco de Baulhe), using railcars for passenger services and steam only on the occasional freight; the impressive Corgo line (Regua to Vila Real and Chaves),

1. A mixed train headed by a Henschel-built 2-8-2T about to leave Sernada for Aviero. (*P. B. Whitehouse*)

2. Henschel-built 0-4-4-0 Mallet tank on waiting-duty turn at Porto Trindade station. (*P. B. Whitehouse*)

3. Henschel 2-8-2T, built in 1931, of Portuguese National Railways at Trindade station in Porto. The narrow-gauge suburban services from Porto Trindade succumbed to diesels from 1977 and so too have services on the group of lines based on Sernada. (*P. B. Whitehouse*)

using 2-4-6-0 Mallet tanks for all its trains, which are mixed; the Tua line (Tua to Mirandela and Braganca), using railcars and 2-6-0 tanks and 0-4-4-0 Mallet tanks on mixed trains; and the Sabor line (Pocinho to Dua Igrejas, for Miranda), using minute railcars and 2-4-6-0 tanks on mixed trains. All these narrow-gauge trains connect with those of the Portuguese State Railways on the Douro Valley line – itself occasionally worked by steam beyond Regua. Then there are the lines which centre on the somewhat remote junction of Sernada da Vouga, where diesels now throb and the once heterogeneous collection of narrow-gauge steam engines is no more. Of them, two run to the Atlantic coast towns of Espinho and Aviero, whilst the third goes east to the cathedral city of Viseu; from there a further branch runs on to Santa Comba Dao.

The motive power used on the Portuguese narrow-gauge system is delightfully various, as is the rolling stock. Certain types and classes are restricted to their own particular lines, and each system or separate line has its own workshops (usually at the main junction point) fully capable of all but the heaviest repairs; for the heavy work, engines are sent to Porto on a low-loader, rather as the Leek & Manifold sent its engines to Crewe

in the good (or bad) old days.

Looking at each of the groups separately we find that over ten years they have had no common locomotive class, though most lines used the small 2-6-0 tank and each had its own form of Mallet tank.

The Porto lines until 1977 used three main classes of tank locomotives: the Henschel-built 0-4-4-0 Mallet of 1905 vintage with really magnificent copper-capped chimneys and sparkling black paintwork; varying makes and classes of 2-6-0 (including Decauville, Kessler, Orenstein, Koppel and Esslingen), most with stove-pipe chimneys, but with some engines dating back to 1886 with copper-capped bellmouths; and the large 1931 smoke-deflectored Henschel 2-8-2 tanks. Unlike the smaller locomotives, the last-named never seened to be turned but ran chimney-first into Porto. All the engines on the Porto system were maintained in the workshops at Boa Vista, between Porto and Senhora da Hora. Once, a British-built Vulcan Foundry 0-4-4-0 Fairlie tank dating back to 1875 ran over the line, ending its days banking heavily overcrowded holiday specials, with surplus passengers clinging happily on to the buffers and drawgear with the good-natured irrepressible air of those clinging to the sides of a Cairo tramcar.

The Douro Valley railways rely, in the

main, on a remarkable wheel arrangement – a 2-4-6-0 Mallet compound tank engine dating from 1911 but some of the redundant 0-4-4-0 Mallet tanks from the Porto area are now in service there. The Henschel 2-4-6-0 engines were introduced as a sensible modification of the more normal 0-6-6-0 tank. The Tamega line runs one engine only at a time, usually one of the odd pair of 0-4-4-0 Mallet tanks, slightly larger than the Porto engines and carrying stove-pipe chimneys. The precipitous, heavily graded and tortuous Corgo line relies solely on the 2-4-6-0 tanks for all its services; as all its trains are mixed, loads are usually heavy even in the quiet season. There are workshops at Regua and the Corgo's copper-cap-chimneyed engines are smartly turned out and a delight to behold. There is, in addition, an old 0-4-0 tank (No E1) which had lain derelict at Regua for many years, and which was recently put through the big works at Campanha – ostensibly for preservation; however, the engine has recently returned to Regua to act as station pilot.

Next up the valley, the Tua line has 2-6-0 and 0-4-4-0 tanks for its few mixed trains and the engines, as well as the railcars used for most passenger turns, are serviced in the small modern shops at Mirandela. Sometimes one can also find one of the small 0-6-0 tanks working on this branch. The last and most remote of these railways, the Sabor, again uses 2-4-6-0 Mallets for its mixed trains, for it is another very steeply graded line. In recent years, one of the Tua Mallets has been the sole example of a Portuguese narrow-gauge engine using the Giesl ejector, with an ugly flat chimney which does not enhance its appearance. The Sabor line workshops are at Pocinho and traffic on this section is at a low ebb.

Somehow, the Sernada da Vouga system has an individuality which is particularly appealing. Its centre at Sernada is almost nowhere, it is the person-ification of an old-time country junction with a wine-shop-cum-café and a locomotive works to boot, and it also had a greater variety of motive power than either of the other two. Locomotives included the 2-6-0 and 2-4-6-0 tanks, but two other classes were unique to the line – they were another Henschel 2-8-2 tank dating from 1924, machines with a very handsome outline and steel ladders running down the sides of their smoke-boxes, and a class of 4-6-0 tanks by Borsig, dating back to 1908. The latter were foreshortened in looks and reminded one very much of some of the locomotives which once worked the lamented Irish 3ft-gauge lines. Quite often engines of each class could be seen working at Sernada at once, generally at the three times during the day when trains from each of the three limbs connected and intershunted, when the station became a sort of Portuguese narrow-gauge Crewe of fifty years ago.

The diesel units, which often run with trailers, are painted in a smart blue, and are of two main types – to the un-technical, large and small! The former are used on the Porto suburban and the Tamega lines, while the diminutive cars that run out of Pocinho seem like bumping juveniles in comparison. Blue is also the colour for the newer steel-bodied passenger stock, though the older coaches more often found on the country systems are painted dark green. Fares are cheap, and you are recommended to travel first class if you intend to go far.

There is one other narrow-gauge system – that of the Porto Docks and Harbour Board. The system was originated back in 1884 when the artificial harbour was made at the mouth of the River Douro. Two long breakwaters were built to protect the man-made port and the metre-gauge railway was constructed to carry the granite used from the quarry of San Gens just outside Porto. Today this little railway is diesel operated. It is rumoured that there are still three spotless and shining Belgian-built steam tank engines tucked away in a shed, waiting either for a buyer or an emergency.

Taken all in all, the metre-gauge railways of Portugal are a delightful anachronism, and under a recent review of their health by the authorities, the lives of the more countrified lines are bound to be limited. The railways run in modest-living country where the general economy is limited and includes few natural resources, so that their first objective was, and must continue to be, the provision of economical transport services for the local regions which they serve. Because of the necessity for economy in their construction, like other similar narrow-gauge railways, they have a tendency to 'go round' rather than 'up and down' and follow the river valleys where possible. There are some examples of tunnelling and bridging, notably on the Porto line and on the Tua railway; on the latter there is one place where the line emerges from a short tunnel parallel to a precipice where it is carried on a bridge built along the rock face, before diving into a further tunnel.

Most of the country lines link the towns and villages along their various river banks and take the seeker of the genuine rural life into terrain full of history and Roman or medieval remains, as well as the more active industry of wine making. This, together with the unusual and interesting variety of tank engines, makes a visit to a lovely land imperative for those who want to see a little of yesterday while it is still left – the motor car will soon bring it to an end.

CP metre-gauge 2-8-2T locomotive and passenger train passing a diesel railcar at Avenida da Franca in May 1968. Although diesel railcars were in use on Porto suburban services in the 1960s another decade passed before steam was finally eliminated in 1977. (*B. Stephenson*)

3

4

1. Norwegian State Railways' (NSB) Bergen-Oslo train headed by class-E1 14 6,900hp electric locomotives at Geilo in September 1972. More than sixty per cent of the NSB is electrified on the 15,000volt single-phase ac system, similar to the systems developed by Sweden and Germany-Austria-Switzerland between the two world wars. (*A. H. Ellis*)

2. Finnish Railways' (VR) 2-8-2 No 1044 leaving Helsinki with a train for Rühimaki in March 1962. The VR system is more akin to that of its eastern neighbour, Russia, sharing its 5ft track gauge, than to those of the other Scandinavian countries to the west. (*F. Firminger*)

3. Danish State Railways' (DSB) locomotive No 959 at Fredericia, on the east coast of the main island, in August 1968, by which time steam was almost at an end on DSB. (*J. E. Bell*)

4. Danish State Railways, like most European systems, started dieselisation in the 1950s. Among the early DSB diesel locomotives was this General Motors AIA-AIA type seen at Copenhagen. Today, apart from Copenhagen suburban 1,500 volt dc electric services, DSB is wholly dieselised, although a main-line electrification plan for the next twenty years is under discussion. (*J. Jaundreli*)

Overleaf: Finnish class-VR1 0-6-0T shunter at Savonlinna. In the days of steam coal was scarce in Finland since it had mostly to be imported. A large number of smaller VR steam locomotives were designed as wood burners, hence the wide spark-arrester chimney. (*J. Toy*)

1

4

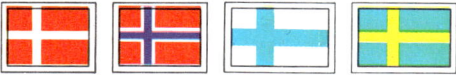

1. Finnish 2-6-2T shunter No 1418 at Seinajoki in July 1968. (*J. E. Bell*)

2 and 3. Massive freight trains in northern Sweden between Kiruna and Narvik (Norway) in the same location in winter and summer. That in 2 is headed by a single ASEA DM3 9,750hp electric locomotive and the other has two ASEA-equipped diode-rectifier locomotives totalling over 14,000hp. Although Narvik is on Norway's west coast it is isolated from the rest of the NSB system. The rail link is worked by Swedish and NSB locomotives which operate through across the border to Kiruna on the route to Boden. (*ASEA: J. C. Cowne*)

4. Norwegian State Railways' electric locomotives emerging from a snow-shed at Myrdal on the Bergen-Oslo line. This line reaches an altitude of 4,250 feet (1,300 metres) in climbing through the mountains to reach the west coast. (*A. H. Ellis*)

2

3

1

3

1. Diesel railcar set of Transandine Railway, partly owned by Chilean State Railways, at Polvaredas, Argentina, in March 1972. (*R. M. Quinn*)

2. A Bolivian 2-8-2 heads a freight at Cochabamba in 1970. (*D. T. Rowe*)

3. Diesel locomotive of Argentine Railways' General San Martin Railway at Palmira in March 1972. (*R. M. Quinn*)

4. Diesel-headed train of Southern Railway of Peruvian Corporation Railways leaving Cuzco in March 1972. (*R. M. Quinn*)

1

2

1. Peruvian Corporation Central of Peru Railway workshops outside Lima in March 1972. (*D. Wennberg*)

2. Chilean State Railways' Alco 2-8-2 locomotive at Antilhue, near the southern end of the South system, in March 1972. (*R. M. Quinn*)

3. FCAB diesel shunter on a La Paz train at Antofagasta in 1968. (*J. N. Westwood*)

4. A Garratt steam locomotive of the Antofagasta line at La Paz-Alta, Bolivia. (*D. T. Rowe*)

5. A modern diesel railcar and a German-built steam locomotive side by side on the Southern line near Cuzco in 1969. (*C. & D. Gannon*)

Spain is well known as one of Europe's favourite playgrounds, and holiday posters are to be seen everywhere extolling her seaside attractions of sunshine and sand, and the marvels of her southern cities such as Seville and Granada. The holiday areas are well defined and neatly labelled Costa del Sol, Costa Brava, etc. The number of tourists flocking to Spain each year is impressive, but the majority travel in package tours, arrive by air, and are concentrated in very limited geographical areas.

All this is a comparatively recent phenomenon and has brought dramatic change to a way of life virtually undisturbed for centuries. Spain's political troubles hindered her development during the first half of this century and economic difficulties after the Second World War (in which she did not take part) further slowed advancement in many fields. Thus, while the railways of many other European countries pressed ahead with modernisation, Spain had neither the foeign aid nor resources of her own to undertake large projects, and had perforce to be content for many years with a policy of 'make do and mend', which barely managed to keep pace with the rate of deterioration evolving from the ravages of the Civil War of 1936-39 and the lack of materials available thereafter.

Although steam survived longer in other countries, it was in Spain that there was a variety of ancient motive power almost to the end of steam traction. In Spain foreign aid and economic recovery provided the wherewithal for one of Europe's most ambitious railway modernisation plans, the RENFE ten-year plan for 1964-73. During this period two main

1

2

3

lines, one of international importance (Madrid-Burgos direct railway), were completed, many important routes elecrified, track and signalling drastically overhauled, rolling stock renewed, and, slightly more recently, steam traction, previously paramount, was finally eliminated.

Railways in Spain began effectively in 1848, when British engineers built the short Barcelona-Mataro Railway. Other lines soon followed, and were built to the wide gauge of 5ft 6in, which was six Castilian feet and had been recommended in a report prepared for the Government in 1844. This decision, which was instrumental in causing neighbouring Portugal also to adopt the broad gauge, has always

1. 0-4-0T 'Odiel' at Corrales on the Tharsis Railway in the Rio Tinto copper-mining area of southern Spain.
(*D. T. Rowe*)

2. Spanish National Railways' (Red Nacional de los Ferrocarriles Españoles: RENFE) 0-8-0 No 040 2184 heading a freight train at Linares in September 1963.
(*D. T. Rowe*)

3. RENFE's 2-6-0 No 130 2142, 'Arboleas', of NBL design, leaving Corca for Baza in September 1963. Spanish (and Portuguese) railways adopted 5ft 6in gauge for the main routes, which has prevented through working by ordinary trains from and to France and beyond except by special arrangements to change wheels and bogies for some stock.
(*D. T. Rowe*)

4. RENFE No 282F 0405, an oil-fuelled Aragon Garratt built by Babcock & Wilcox in 1930 and withdrawn in 1969. RENFE, alone among the mainland European railways, had several Garratt articulated locomotives. (*D. T. Rowe*)

made through rail connection with the rest of Europe difficult, although it has been overcome to some extent by using wagons (and recently passenger coaches) which are converted at the frontier.

Historically, the high cost of construction contributed to the authorisation of a large network of narrow-gauge railways, mostly metre, which, when they were of more than local importance, were also inconvenient for the nationwide transport of freight, fruit in particular requiring quick transit and minimum handling. By 1900 there were about 7,100 miles of broad-gauge and 1,450 miles of narrow-gauge railways, and many of the small broad-gauge companies were being absorbed into larger ones. In time this process resulted in two companies emerging to control a large area of the country. The two almost equally matched concerns were the Madrid, Zaragoza & Alicante Railway (MZA) and the Norte Railway. Behind them came the Andaluces Company which, however, never gained complete ascendency in the south, where small companies, some British financed, abounded until the formation of one national railway system for the broad gauge.

The single authority was formed in 1941 with the creation of the Red Nacional de los Ferrocarriles Españoles (RENFE), which took over around 8,000 miles of broad-gauge track and over 3,000 steam locomotives. Some of the locomotives dated back almost to the first years of railways in the country; they were of such great variety that visitors from almost every locomotive-building country in Europe (including Russia) and North America could find some of their

national products in action. New locomotives were built, but few withdrawals took place as traffic grew constantly; after a few pioneer enthusiasts had visited the country in the early 1950s tales trickled back of the wonderful machines still active and other fans set out on a pilgrimage quite different from those who for centuries had travelled to other Spanish shrines, such as that of Santiago de Compostela.

The new saints were locomotives a hundred or more years old; their shrines the steamy depots of junctions like Miranda de Ebro, on the windswept Castilian plain, and the rain-sodden industrial valleys of Asturias, where coal mines provided a selection of little railways not at all like those touristic ones in Wales as they are today, though sometimes in rather similar terrain. As the enthusiasts grew more numerous, they pentrated into remote valleys, until, to add to the stocklists of the broad-gauge RENFE, there came booklets on the industrial and minor railways of various areas. With the decline of steam even the RENFE, which had always been sympathetic to railfans, took to publishing lists of withdrawals and details of where certain types could be found.

The oldest active class of steam locomotives in Spain when the RENFE was formed in 1941, and still going strong on shunting duties until the mid-1960s, were some 0-6-0 tender engines built by Kitson, Thompson and Hewitson at the Railway Foundry Leeds in 1857-58 and by Cail of Paris in 1858. To the end they remained almost as built, some having had rough wooden cabs added while the original 'weatherboard' or 'spectacle

1. Locomotive-cleaning operations on shed at Ponferrada, in September 1971. (*A. G. Orchard*)

2. Wooden two-tiered train with locomotive No 230 2088 arriving at Valencia terminus in September 1961. Although such antique double-deck coaches are no longer in service, modern double-deck suburban coaches are increasingly a feature of east European countries. (*L. King*)

3. Westbound goods train on the Zaragoza-Miranda de Ebro line near San Felices headed by RENFE 4-8-0 No 240F 2556 in May 1968. (*B. Stephenson*)

4. JOP Huelva Railway's No 5, an 0-4-0 tank engine built by the German firm Orenstein & Koppel. (*D. T. Rowe*)

plate' remained in place. In Spain, unusually, the shunters and tank engines, not the fine modern express locomotives, carried names, some of them historic, such as *Isobel la Catolica* (I doubt if *she* would have been amused) *Alfonso VIII* and *El Cid* (stationed at Valencia, of course). Others were named after towns and rivers, and one, perhaps aptly, *Terrible.*

Passing from the huge variety of 0-6-0s and 0-8-0s to the larger types, Spain always had a large proportion of eight-coupled machines, including many 4-8-0s and 4-8-2s. The Mountains class (4-8-2s) was perpetuated by the RENFE and in production up to 1952, when the standard mixed-traffic engine selected as

successor and built in large numbers up to 1960 was a 2-8-2 of North British design. Latterly, these modern types were built for oil firing, and older types were converted from coal, which in Spain is of indifferent quality.

Tank engines have never been numerous in Spain; one little 0-4-0T now preserved in Madrid came from the FC Urbano de Jerez, the sherry town where legend has it that at the annual festival the boiler was filled with wine instead of water! Many tank engine classes consisted of one or two machines only, from small concerns like the Mollet-Caldas and Cinco Casas-Tomelloso railways, although a batch of 4-8-4Ts, built in Barcelona in 1923-24 was distributed to various lines under State control.

Spain had a great variety of articulated locomotives quite unequalled in Europe. Mallet compound tender locomotives came first, built for the Central of Aragon Railway in 1906, 1912 and 1927-28, the more recent ones still being active around Valencia in 1969. Some Kitson-Meyers went to the Great Southern of Spain in 1908 but were withdrawn in 1953. Garratts were introduced in 1930 by the Central of Aragon for express passenger working between Valencia and Calatayud. Six were built by Euskalduna at Bilbao and latterly they were used on the very heavy Seville-Barcelona through train between Valencia and Tarragona. They were the only Garratts used on passenger trains in Europe, although this is quite common practice in Africa. These passenger Garratts were of 4-6-2+2-6-4 wheel arrangement, but in 1930 the same operator had six 2-8-2+2-8-2 Garratts built by Babcock & Wilcox at Bilbao for freight traffic. Until the RENFE built some Santa Fe (2-10-2) machines for coal traffic around Leon in 1942, these last-mentioned Garratts were the most powerful steam locomotives in the Iberian peninsula. Most surprisingly, as late as 1961 the RENFE had a further six very similar Garratts built; they were the last large steam locomotives built for service in Western Europe.

It is a fact that until the end of steam the RENFE continued developing this form of traction. Although the 1961 Garratts were the last steam locomotives built in Spain, they were essentially repeat orders of a well-tried design, but in 1956 the RENFE had put into service ten express passenger 4-8-4s of a new design and the only tender locomotives of this wheel arrangement in the country. They were built for heavy international trains between the French frontier and Madrid, and worked the non-electrified section between Alsasua and Avila. This main artery was gradually electrified under the 1964-73 plan and the fine machines were relegated to freight duties.

Modern developments were not neglected, and several standard 2-8-2s and a 4-8-0 were fitted with Giesl ejectors, while there was one experiment with a Franco-Crosti boiler on a 2-8-0. Under the ten-year plan, steam was expected to be extinct by 1973, but it lingered on until 1975. The RENFE is certainly not unaware of the historic value of its locomotives, and some have been put aside for preservation, along with interesting coaching stock and other relics.

This brief look at the steam stock of the RENFE only touches on a vast subject and mention of many types has perforce been omitted. Although in the early days locomotives came from abroad, Spanish industry was building 4-8-2s in 1925 and after the Civil and World Wars local industry expanded as fast as was possible under difficult conditions. Steam locomotives were built by La Maquinista Terrestre y Maritima (MTM) of Barcelona, Babcock & Wilcox and Euskalduna, both of Bilbao and Devis (later Macosa) of Valencia. In steam days these companies built solely for the Spanish market (apart from an isolated batch of Spanish type 4-8-0s for Portugal), but today Macosa and the Bilbao firms export diesels to South American countries.

Turning to the narrow-gauge railways of Spain, these have ranged from local roadside tramway-type lines to electrified main lines operating Pullman cars. Most of the former category are now extinct, especially all those charming little lines of sub-metric gauge — 60 and 75cm. Particularly interesting were the 75cm Veldepeñas-Puertollano Railway, with 0-6-0 tender engines, and the Onda-Castellon line of the same gauge which passed through the town streets and paused briefly in the main square of Castellon de la Plana before being given right of way at the road junction by the policeman on traffic duty! The last of the 75cm lines to go was San Feliu-Gerona, closed only a few years ago, and probably unnoticed by the holiday crowds at this quite well-known Costa Brava resort. Publicity could perhaps have made it a tourist attraction, but it died mourned only by a few local people, steam worked to the last by 0-6-2Ts, some of the engines built for the opening of the line in 1892.

On the metre gauge, closures have included many of the lesser isolated lines, but at least one, Malaga-Fuengirola, closed not because of lack of traffic, but because it was converted to the broad gauge! And up along the northern coastline a long metre-gauge link, under construction for many years, has now been completed and it is possible to travel from Hendaye, across the border in France, over 500 miles to El Ferrol, via Bilbao, Santander and Oviedo. It is along Spain's northern coastline that the narrow gauge is strongest, with electric traction between the French frontier and Bilbao since the 1920s, and nowadays fast diesel railcar services thereafter. In the heyday of steam, a decade or so ago, the trains between Bilbao, Santander and Oviedo were hauled by steam, Engerth-type machines of the Cantabrico, and tank engines of the Economicos de Asturias, all bright green with polished brass nameplates.

On the inland Robla railway, old American Baldwin 2-8-0s rubbed shoulders with ex-Swiss Rhaetian Railway machines of the same wheel arrangement, while metre-gauge Garratts with long names hauled the heaviest coal trains. This railway worked its daily through passenger train with fine green Pacifics, sold by Tunisia to be scrapped in the furnaces of Bilbao but rescued and given a new lease of life by the Robla. Other ex-Tunisian types also saw service in Spain, some 2-10-0s on the Peñarroya-Puertollano line and Mallett tank engines on the Utrillas railway serving Zaragoza. Metre-gauge Garratts were in Catalonia on the long line up into the mountains, and there was a 3ft 6in-gauge pair on the Rio Tinto mining line near Huelva.

Tender Mallets and more Garratts saw service on the long mineral line from the Ojos Negros mine to Sagunto Steelworks near Valencia. Replaced by diesels, the whole railway was closed and traffic diverted over the nearby broad-gauge RENFE, once the Central of Aragon road of the Garratts and Mallets. At the other end of the scale, many railways had little

British-built 4-4-0Ts from Falcon of Loughborough, and the Alcoy-Gandia railway near Valencia had a stud of Beyer Peacock 2-6-2Ts in 1890-91, which lasted until closure of the railway a few years ago. When funds were low they sold one to the Sagunto Steelworks and kept going with the rest!

Even more remarkable, the Sestao-Galdames Company, an ore line near Bilbao, did not buy a new loco since 1877, and in the 1960s its shed was full of the cannibalised remains of the two types still in use, Kitson 4-6-0Ts of 1873-74 and Manning Wardle 0-6-0Ts of 1873-77, but this railway has the unusual gauge of 3ft 9¼in. Unusual gauges have abounded in Spain. The 4ft Tharsis railway shares its gauge only with the Glasgow underground, and since it was built by a Glasgow company perhaps that is no coincidence! The island of Mallorca is exclusively 3ft (nowhere else in Spain is) while the European standard gauge of 4ft 8½in is to be found only on metros, one Barce-

lona suburban line and the Langreo Railway, one of the oldest in the country.

Not so long ago, locomotives of three gauges could be seen in the same shed at the Poveda Sugar Factory and at the Cuatro Vientos air force establishment, both near Madrid, the gauges being 60cm, 1m and 5ft 6in. On the metre gauge serving the Sugar Factory were tender Mallets built in Belgium and the broad-gauge shunter at the factory was a 4-4-0T of the type built by Beyer Peacock for the British Metropolitan Railway of London. Another of this type remained in use until it was withdrawn recently for preservation at the Basconia Steelworks, Bilbao. The locomotives came originally from the Bilbao-Tudela Railway and were sold out of service long before the formation of the RENFE.

Today, much of the metre gauge still exists, but in modernised form, with diesel or electric traction, although a few steam locomotives survive here and there, particularly in industrial use. The one railway which is still entirely steam

1. A RENFE standard-gauge diesel-hydraulic locomotive heads the 'Catalan' Talgo out of Geneva. The Talgo-type train, consisting of short lightweight coaches articulated on single axle wheelsets, is used in Europe only by RENFE. The 'Catalan' runs through between Barcelona and Geneva with automatic adjustment of wheel width for the change of gauge at Port Bou. The RENFE locomotives no longer work outside Spain. ('La Vie du Rail')

2. Electric multiple-unit trains of Bilbao Railways and Suburban Transport in June 1968. (B. Stephenson)

worked in 1978 is Ponferrada-Villablino situated on the old main line from Madrid to Galicia beyond Leon, where locomotives include the last Engerths still active, Baldwin-built 2-6-2Ts of 1919 and Spanish 2-6-0s, the most recent of which was built in 1956. Its future is far from secure, however, and anyone interested should lose no time in paying the line a visit.

1. The Gotthard line abounds in bridges, viaducts and tunnels. This is the Lower Meienreuss bridge near Wassen on the northern ramp. (*Swiss Federal Railways*)

2. One of the original trains of the Jungfrau Railway, recently replaced by modern units. The Jungfrau Railway reaches a summit of 11,300 feet (3,454 metres) at Jungfraujoch station, the highest (but in a tunnel) in Europe. (*G. M. Kichenside*)

3. Swiss Federal Railways' contribution to the Trans-Europe Express network in the 1960s was a class of five-car (later six-car) four-voltage luxury electric multiple-units. (*John Adams*)

4. Meeting point at Kleine-Scheidegg at 6,760 feet (2,060 metres) altitude and overlooking Grindelwald of the Wengernalp Railway and the Jungfrau Railway. (*G. M. Kichenside*)

5. Tank locomotive No 1 of the Brienz-Rothorn rack railway at Brienz in the Swiss Bernese Oberland. (*J. M. Boyes*)

Following spread: RhB class G4/5 2-8-0 locomotive with an excursion train in May 1967 on the Rhätische Bahn (Rhaetian Railway) near Klosters, Switzerland. This and its sister locomotive were originally kept for emergency reserve use but were brought out for excursions in the late 1960s. Unfortunately, when heavy boiler repairs are needed the boilers have to be sent to Germany as Swiss firms cannot undertake the work. (*B. Stephenson*)

4

1. Metre-gauge Furka Oberalp Railway HGe 4/4 rack-and-adhesion electric locomotive on the Grengiols viaduct with a Brig to Chur train in the Rhône Valley in May 1967. (*B. Stephenson*)

2. A Gotthard freight at the Lower Waltinger bridge near Wassen. (*Swiss Federal Railways*)

3. Berne-Lötschberg-Simplon Ae 8/8 double-unit electric locomotive passing Kandergrund station southbound towards the nine-mile-long Lötschberg tunnel with a goods train. (*W. R. G. van den Brock*)

4 and 5. Two views of one of the two veteran steam locomotives of the Vitznau-Rigi Railway (VRB), No 17, at the lakeside station and on the climb of the Rigi. The VRB, opened in 1871, is Europe's oldest rack-and-pinion mountain railway. Although electrified since the 1930s the steam locomotives are still used for special excursions. (*G. M. Kichenside*)

6. Two of the Pilatus rack railway's cars at the Alpnachstad terminus in May 1967. With a gradient of 1 in 2, this is Europe's steepest rack line and has the special Locher rack rail with teeth on each side. (*B. Stephenson*)

4. ▲

5. ▼

6

3

1. Turkish State Railways' (TCDD) class-DE20 1,980hp diesel electric. Modernisation of the TCDD started later than in most European countries and has not proceeded so rapidly. In the early 1970s steam still outnumbered other types of locomotive by six to one. (*C. J. Gammell*)

2. One of the 4,000hp 25kV Bo-Bo electric locomotives supplied to Turkish State Railways by the 50-cycle European group, at Halkali. On deciding to electrify certain routes, the TCDD, having for many years been equipped by European manufacturers, chose to follow latest French practice with 50-cycle 25kV material. (*C. J. Gammell*)

3. Turkey has always been cosmopolitan in its choice of steam locomotives. After the Second World War it was possible to see engines built in Britain, France, Germany, USA and Czechoslovakia. This is a German-built (Maffei) 2-6-2WT at Mersin on the Baghdad Railway in September 1969. (*I. Krause*)

4. Electric multiple-unit set on suburban service on the Istanbul 25kV system. (*C. M. Whitehouse*)

Overleaf: The last remaining TCDD narrow-gauge line near Samsun, on the Black Sea, with a train from Carsamba in September 1969. Four 2-6-0 tank engines were built specially for the line by Henschel in 1924, one of which is seen here. (*I. Krause*)

4

The three pictures on this page represent relatively modern Turkish steam power, all 2-10-0s, built in three different countries.

1. Czech-built (Skoda) 2-10-0 on an express passenger train at Irmak in May 1970. (*T. B. Owen*)

2. Spotlessly turned out German-built 'Kriegslok' 2-10-0 on an express passenger train in October 1969. (*C. J. Gammell*)

3. TCDD Vulcan Ironworks (USA) 2-10-0 No 56356 heading a goods train south from Kayseri. (*T. B. Owen*)

Britain was the home of the steam locomotive and it is fitting that the first part of the United Kingdom section of this book should be devoted to steam locomotives preserved either on privately run independent tourist railways, or in museums, or for operation on BR.

1. Talyllyn Railway 2ft 3in-gauge 0-4-0WT No 6, 'Douglas' at Towyn Wharf station in September 1968. The Talyllyn, rescued in 1950, was the first of the preserved railways in Britain. (*John Adams*)

2. GWR-type Castle-class 4-6-0 No 7029, 'Clun Castle', at Cricklewood in 1969 – a 1950 double-chimney type preserved by the Clun Castle Trust. (*M. Pope*)

Overleaf: Steam in action on the Keighley & Worth Valley Railway in Yorkshire, but seen here disguised for filming 'The Railway Children'. A former Great Western 0-6-0 pannier tank lettered GNSRY (Great Northern & Southern Railway) heads a third-class coach from the Metropolitan Railway and two North Eastern Railway saloons. (*R. Bastin*)

1. Famous ex-LNER A3 Pacific 'Flying Scotsman' near Gargrave, on the Midland line, with a special train in March 1968. This engine is one of those in private hands which is passed to run on special BR excursions over selected routes. BR is allowing steam excursions to run on its lines until at least 1985 and in 1978 started to run steam trips of its own. (*A. Stewart*)

2. Dart Valley Railway 45XX-class 2-6-2T No 4555 on a train at Buckfastleigh in September 1970. The DVR operates regular steam trains on both the Buckfastleigh and Paignton-Kingswear lines as tourist attractions in south Devon. (*C. J. Gammell*)

3. Preserved by the Wight Locomotive Society, O2 No 24 'Calbourne' in immediate pre-war SR 'Sunshine' lettering style, at Havenstreet in September 1971. Gradually the company formed to operate steam trains at Havenstreet has been opening more of the line towards Newport. (*G. M. Kichenside*)

1. Ex-LMS Jubilee-class 4-6-0 No 5593 'Kolhapur' photographed outside the Standard Gauge Steam Trust depot. (*P. B. Whitehouse*)

2. Representative of a class of some seventy Adams 4-4-2T engines on the London & South Western Railway from 1882. No 488 had various owners and numbers until it was bought after withdrawal by BR (No 30583) in 1961 by the Bluebell Line, where it now works in LSWR 1918 livery. (*M. Pope*)

3. Festiniog Railway 'Fairlie' articulated 0-4-4-0T 'Earl of Merioneth' at Porthmadog. The driver and fireman stand on each side of the boiler and central firebox. (*M. Pope*)

1. Typical BR train of the Scottish Highlands routes in the 1970s. Class-27 D5356 crosses River Lochy with a Fort William-Mallaig train in 1971. (*D. Cross*)

2. British Railways' High Speed Train No 253008. (*British Railways Board*)

Republic of Ireland

1. No A58R, a GM-powered Metrovick diesel-electric locomotive, heading an express passenger train at Mallow in July 1968. (*R. C. Flewitt*)

2. GS & W 0-6-0 No 186 on an excursion near Listowel in June 1972. (*C. J. Gammell*)

3. First of CIE's new air-conditioned trains which entered service between Dublin and Cork in 1972. The coaches were built by British Rail Engineering. (*Coras Iompair Eireann*)

1. Union Pacific 4-12-2 No 9032, a rare American three-cylinder engine, at Topeka, Kansas, in mid 1952. (*J. M. Jarvis*)

2. Brand-new EMD (GM) diesel locomotives heading the Santa Fe 'Super Chief' at Chicago Dearborn in mid 1952. American diesels of this period were generally formed of several units, the middle ones of which had no driving cabs and were controlled in multiple from the end driving units. (*J. M. Jarvis*)

3. Denver & Rio Grande Western 'California Zephyr' ready for departure behind five GM F units at Denver Union station in June 1969. (*V. Goldberg*)

4. Fine action picture of New York Central's 'Empire State' express at Dunkirk, New York, when steam still ruled. (*J. M. Jarvis*)

1

2

3

4

1. A 750hp Baldwin D5 4-4-750, No 52 of California Western RR, built in 1949 and scrapped in 1970, seen here at Fort Bragg in August 1969. (*J. K. Hayward*)

2. Norfolk & Western class-J 4-8-4 No 605 on the 'Powhattan Arrow' (Norfolk to Cincinnati) in New River gorge near Ripplemead, Virginia, in September 1951. (*J. M. Jarvis*)

3. Chicago Transit Authority car on the 'Skokie Swift' service at Skokie, Illinois, in September 1964. (*J. K. Hayward*)

4. Milwaukee Road Pacific No 165 leaving Chicago with a local train in summer 1952. (*J. M. Jarvis*)

5. Modern diesel locomotives Nos 3041 and 3042 of the Illinois Central RR. (*Illinois Central Railroad*)

6. Norfolk & Western 2-8-8-4 Mallet on coal empties in New River Gorge in September 1951. Mallets were articulated locomotives in which the leading driving wheel and cylinder units were carried in a pivoted subframe, while the rear wheels and cylinders were rigidly mounted in the main frame which also carried the boiler. (*J. M. Jarvis*)

7. Milwaukee Road Mallet 2-6-6-2 on the 'Olympic Hiawatha' train at Tacoma, Washington, in July 1952. (*J. M. Jarvis*)

1. The Burlington Northern (Northern Pacific) 'North Coast Limited' at Livingstone in July 1970. Until this time each US railroad ran its own passenger services, but, soon after, a new national organisation, AMTRAK, took over responsibility for long-distance passenger operation in the USA contracting with the individual railways for stock and locomotives. (*V. Goldberg*)

2. Diesel-hauled 'City of San Francisco' in Echo Canyon in the late 1950s. (*Union Pacific RR*)

3. Union Pacific 4-8-4 at Cheyenne in September 1969. (*P. B. Whitehouse*)

4. Chicago & North Western Pacific No 1650 at Milwaukee in mid 1952. (*J. M. Jarvis*)

5. Southern Pacific 0-6-0 switcher (shunter) No 1268 at San Francisco in mid 1952. (*J. M. Jarvis*)

6. Amtrak Metroliner awaiting departure from Washington Union station for New York in October 1972. (*J. K. Hayward*)

121

Federal Republic of Germany

German steam locomotives have always been among the most impressive in Europe; in their last years they attracted even more attention, owing to the very sensible policy of the Federal Railway (Deutsche Bundesbahn) in keeping its more efficient machines at work as an interim measure pending the completion of electrification – which in turn released the limited number of diesels to take over steam workings. Yet German steam, as we have known it in the past ten years or so, is basically the result of two quite recent decisions by the State railway authorities; during the nineteenth and early twentieth centuries, the steam locomotives of Germany were as eccentric and mixed a bag as ever ran on a country's railways.

Historically speaking, the first German steam locomotive was an oddity built by the Königlichen Eisengiesserei (Royal Ironworks) at Berlin in Prussia in the year 1815, but it was only experimental and never came to anything. Certainly when the first true railway opened, in 1835, between Nuremburg and Fürth, in Bavaria, its locomotive, as so often with such lines, was a Stephenson design imported from England complete with top-hatted driver. That worthy, William Wilson, settled down with a German wife; his engine, *Der Adler*, settled down to haul Bavarian goods and people, and the various little kingdoms that then made up 'Germany' settled down to build their own railways and motive power.

The early locomotives were much like others of their era, light four- and six-coupled machines for the most part and barely adequate for their jobs. It was not until the rise of Prussia and, eventually, the formation of the German Empire in 1871 that any real pattern emerged. Prussia had always believed in State railways and gradually the other major States acquired, from private companies, or built their own systems. They were the so-called Länderbahnen, the State railways of Baden, Bavaria, Oldenburg, Prussia-Hesse, Saxony, and Württemberg, whose only real private rival was the Friedrich-Franz Railway in Mecklenburg.

Oldenburg, Baden and Württemberg were always comparatively small and undistinguished systems but the others developed some distinctive locomotive types and styles. That too was the era of the big famous locomotive firms, such as the Saxon Locomotive Company of Chemnitz, Henschel of Kassel, Krauss-Maffei (an amalgamation) of Munich, Borsig and Schwartzkopff of Berlin, Orenstein & Koppel, and Hanomag (the Hannover Maschinenbau – which speaks for itself). All were innovators in their own right, producing such new ideas as the Krauss-Helmholtz truck for shortening a rigid wheelbase, and developing superheated boilers – to name only two examples.

Thus, during the first decade or so of the twentieth century, an increasing number of standard designs came into being; foremost were probably Prussia and her neighbour Saxony, with their carefully chosen classes to deal with all eventualities. The Saxon State railways administration was probably motivated almost entirely by a desire for internal efficiency; its locomotives were designed specifically for Saxon conditions. Prussia, on the other hand, had designs on other countries and its railways were from the start laid out to allow rapid and unimpeded movement of troops to any point of the compass. Prussian locomotives, even at an early stage, were in keeping with that policy, being deliberately designed so as to be able to run within other people's loading gauges.

The final flowering of that highly Teutonic thoroughness can be seen in the magnificent – for their period – standard passenger and goods classes that appeared from 1910 on. They included the

1. Class-03 Pacific No 03 244 leaving Cochem, Moselle Valley, with a Saarbrücken-Cologne express in August 1964. (*B. Stephenson*)

2. Deutsche Bundesbahn 2-10-0 No 044 277-2 between Punderich and Wengerohr in the Moselle Valley in September 1971. (*R. Bastin*)

1. DB class-038 (originally the Prussian P8) 4-6-0 at Ulm with a Sigmaringen train in May 1967. (*B. Stephenson*)

2. German Federal Railway (DB) class-050 2-10-0 at Horb, in the Black Forest, in May 1971. (*G. R. Hounsell*)

Following spread: A class-052 wartime austerity engine crosses the bridge at Bullay on the Moselle Valley line. (*D. R. Stopher*)

immortal P8 4-6-0, its goods counterparts, the 0-8-0s, 2-8-0s and 0-10-0s of classes G8-10 and the various corresponding tank engines; all took full advantage of the domestic loading gauge available, but the cab roofs were partly demountable and the tall chimneys were in two parts so that the top half could be unbolted to reduce overall height.

These Prussian machines, produced in large numbers for the German effort in the First World War, and later scattered over

half Europe as war reparations, were the first really important landmark in German locomotive design – designs that concentrated on simplicity and efficiency. Of course there were some very handsome prestige locomotives on the other German State systems – high-wheeled Atlantics and, later, some really fine Pacifics – and some might argue that they have been slighted unjustly.

The fact is that apart from the prestige machines, some specialised rack locomotives for the thirteen main-line rack sections around the country, and for a gaggle of rather jolly light railway locomotives in Bavaria, the designs of other States were not really significant in the long run. They certainly included some unusual machines, including Mallets, Meyers and, on the narrow gauge, even the odd Fairlie, and just as certainly contributed largely to the 350 or so classes taken over when the national railway company, the Deutsche Reichsbahn, was formed after the First World

War, but the number in each individual class was rarely high and few were perpetuated.

Modern German steam power dates, in fact, from the formation of the Reichsbahn in 1921. The new national company found itself in dire straits, much of the best Länderbahnen equipment having been taken by others as war reparations and it therefore initiated an urgent programme of standard locomotive construction to make up the losses. It made sense to concentrate on a few efficient classes to help cut complexity and speed production and, inevitably, the newest Prussian standard designs proved most suitable. Only a really powerful Pacific design was missing from the Prussian list and so the magnificent Bavarian locomotives of Class S3/6 were chosen to fill the gap. Otherwise the T3 and T9 branch engines, the P8 4-6-0 and its 4-6-4T counterpart the T18, the G8 series of 0-8-0s and 2-8-0s, the P10 2-8-2 fast passenger locomotive, and the 2-10-0

2

heavy freight machine of Class G12 were adopted virtually unchanged and ordered in large numbers. They sealed the fate of the multitude of elderly Länderbahn designs still ambling about on their own systems, although in the short term the older machines had to be catered for and the new numbering system had to take them into account.

The numbering business was studied with true Prussian thoroughness; not for them the slightly haphazard British plan of starting at number one and working up to 99,999 (with a duplicate list to take care of the oddities). The DR plan was logical simplicity itself once one got to know it. First, a two-figure serial number was allocated to each particular traffic type, running from 01 to 99. The serials were:

01-19 Express tender locomotives
20-39 Slow train locomotives (mixed-traffic type)
40-59 Freight locomotives
60-79 Passenger tank locomotives (in-

cluding mixed traffic)
80-96 Freight tank locomotives
97 Rack locomotives
98 Light railway locomotives
99 Narrow-gauge locomotives (several States, notably Saxony and Württemberg, had been very fond of narrow-gauge branch lines).

Both standard machines and locomotives of similar size, shape and power from various Länderbahnen could well be grouped under the same type number (e.g. Type 89 (0-6-0T) included, besides others, the 'standard' Prussian T8, the Saxon VT – itself in two varieties – the Württemberg T3 and Bavaria's D11, R3/3 classes). The system differentiated between them by allocating to each a batch of three- or four-figure running numbers, the individual number being separated from the type cipher by a gap, e.g. 89 001. For the purposes of stock control, the first figure of the number, or the first two figures of a four-figure number, were added to the type cipher as an index to

form the Class or Baureihe (BR). Thus 89^0 was the standard machine, 89^{81} the Bavarian Class DV numbered 89 8101-10. Where a class was big, the index showed inclusive batches; thus 89^{70-75} covered various batches of the ubiquitous Prussian T3 class.

Having more or less sorted out the bewildering variety of locomotive types, the original Deutsche Reichsbahn became virtually bankrupt in the 1923 depression, although not before it had initiated a much more detailed long-term study of possible future standard locomotive designs. Its successor, a wholly government-controlled concern also known as the Reichsbahn, picked up where the DR left off and developed the study into practical designs for a complete range of standard types (Einheitslokomotiven): these, in essence, were intended to replace all earlier varieties, that formed the basis of DB steam power right up to the end.

The first fruits of the new Reichsbahn's

125

Also of some importance, but with their development cut short by the Second World War, were the improved streamlined Pacifics of BR 01^{10} and 03^{10} that hauled the prestige trains in the late 1930s. Otherwise, classes were again in small numbers only for specialised jobs: they comprised the 06 4-8-4 express locomotives – in prototype form; the twenty-eight BR 45 2-10-2 freight machines which were the heaviest locomotives to run over the DR, and a collection of tank locomotives of various shapes and sizes. Ironically one of the smallest classes, the ten 0-6-0T of BR 89, became one of the most famous through being chosen for a Märklin model in the company's cheapest sets. Most interesting of all, perhaps, was the original BR 23. It was a 2-6-2 version of the Class 50 goods, designed to replace the ageing Prussian P8s, now reclassed as BR 38. Its development was terminated by the war after only two examples had been built and the BR 38 reigned supreme for

Once again Germany lost the war, and once again the railways found themselves in urgent need of motive power to replace war-damaged machines and those removed as reparations.

Fortunately the existing designs were both simple and highly competent machines so that production could quickly be resumed. The life of many Prussian veterans was prolonged, some of the more exotic streamliners, in particular the 01^{10} and 03^{10}, were rebuilt, and more 2-10-0s continued to come off the production lines. Although only one design, a new BR 23 2-6-2, was produced in significant numbers, experiments were continued with various types up to the late 1950s and the locomotive testing centre at Minden became famous for its work in the improvement of locomotive design. The BR 23, incidentally, was intended to replace the veteran P8 but a change of policy prevented further steam locomotive development and when number 23 105 came off the production line, steam locomotive building for the West German railways came to an end. The new German Federal Railway (Deutsche Bundesbahn) decided on a very rational programme of electrification and dieselisation to meet its future motive power requirements and started slowly running down the stock of existing steam power which came to an end in 1977.

policy came in 1925 with the superb Pacifics of Classes 01 (simple) and 02 (compound). They were built for purposes of direct comparison, the simple locomotive winning and subsequently being produced in large numbers; the ten 02s were later converted to simple expansion, as were the ten 04 light compound Pacifics built in 1930 as a comparison with the 03 class light (simple expansion) Pacific.

The standard locomotive policy took effect from 1925 onwards in two major plans. The first one included, besides the basic Pacific designs, a heavy 2-10-0 goods locomotive built in two versions, the Baureihe 44 and 43, a light 2-6-0 (BR 24) for branch line work and a very fine mixed-traffic 2-8-2T (BR 86) which was built in great numbers. Apart from BR 64 (520 built) and BR 80 (39), other classes were built only in small numbers – twenty or fewer – and were mainly for specialised purposes. They comprised BR 62, a 4-6-4T express tank engine design; BR 64, a light 2-6-2T; BR 80, an 0-6-0T shunter; BR 81, an 0-8-0T for local goods work; BR 85 a massive 2-10-2T intended as a banker for the former rack sections which had been converted to adhesion; BR 87 a flexible-wheelbase 0-10-0T for sharp curved lines, and three designs for the narrow gauge under the BR 99 classification. It should be mentioned that Class 43 was a two-cylinder variant of the three-cylinder BR 44 and, when the latter proved successful, was built only in small quantities.

This collection of classes left some very obvious gaps in the stud, which during the 1930s were gradually filled. The most significant designs were the 2-8-2 fast goods locomotives of BR 41, a very fine machine of which 366 were built, the light Pacifics of 03 for lightly laid routes, and the (soon to be ubiquitous) BR 50 'light' 2-10-0 goods locomotives for secondary routes.

another thirty years.

There were also several experimental classes especially for express work including a most unusual prototype 2-8-2 in which pairs of high-speed steam motors drove each coupled axle. Most experimental work, however, was brought to an end by the war and production was concentrated on simple and easily produced types, notably the heavy and light 2-10-0s which themselves were further simplified and from 1942-on were built in huge numbers as the *Kriegsloks* (war locomotives) of Classes 42 and 52. They were the equivalent of our Austerity machines and penetrated into every corner of German-occupied territory. Some even acquired massive condensing tenders, similar to those adopted by the South African Railways, for travelling over the Russian wastes. More common was that peculiarly German device the tender with a guard's hut built into it, which with fully fitted stock obviated the need for guard's vans.

1. No 01 1057 three-cylinder oil-fired Pacific taking a Norddeich-Cologne train towards Ensdetton in April 1969. (B. Stephenson)

2. DB class-V60 diesel shunter on pilot duty at Hof station in May 1967. (B. Stephenson)

3. DB class-042 oil-fuelled 2-8-2 approaching Rheine with a goods train on the Emden-Munster line in April 1969. (B. Stephenson)